Conducting Business Across Borders

Conducting Business Across Borders

Effective Communication in English with Non-Native Speakers

Adrian Wallwork

BEP BUSINESS EXPERT PRESS

Conducting Business Across Borders: Effective Communication in English with Non-Native Speakers

First published in 2018 by
Business Expert Press, LLC
222 East 46th Street, New York, NY 10017
www.businessexpertpress.com

ISBN-13: 978-1-63157-807-6 (paperback)
ISBN-13: 978-1-63157-808-3 (e-book)

Business Expert Press Corporate Communication Collection

Collection ISSN: 2156-8162 (print)
Collection ISSN: 2156-8170 (electronic)

Cover and interior design by Exeter Premedia Services Private Ltd., Chennai, India

First edition: 2018

10 9 8 7 6 5 4 3 2 1

Printed in the United States of America.

Abstract

Most misunderstandings boil down to language—how we use words and how we say them. If this is true within our own language, when we communicate across cultures the problem becomes far more critical. However, because we know we are of different cultures, we tend to blame misunderstandings on differences in culture, ignoring the fact that we may simply have misinterpreted what the other person has said to us, or we may not have been clear in what we said to that person.

This book explains how to communicate in English with non-native speakers in a way that should minimize such misunderstandings. For non-native speakers, communicating with native speakers is a stressful and difficult process. Few native speakers make concessions, in terms of vocabulary used and speed of delivery, so that non-native speakers are left feeling bewildered, frustrated, humiliated, and with a slight (generally unconscious) feeling of inferiority that they have been unable to understand what has been said.

Chapter 1 discusses the dangers of stereotyping and the key difficulties non-natives have with the way mother tongue speakers communicate in English. Chapters 2 and 3 focus on written English and readability, particularly in emails and reports. Chapter 4 covers the elements of the way you speak that may impede on successful communication. Chapters 5 and 6 cover meetings and negotiations; and giving presentations and demos, respectively. Chapter 7 focuses on the use of translation, translators and interpreters. The social side of business communication is discussed in the closing chapter.

Keywords

business, cross cultural communication, culture, EFL, English, ESL, interpreters, languages, meetings, native speakers, negotiations, non-native speakers, presentations, socializing, stereotyping, translation

Contents

Acknowledgments

The following authors, researchers, professors, friends and family members contributed to this book:

Adriano Prosperi, Alex Lamb, Andrea Ceccolini, Angus Brogdon, Antonio Solano, Begum Cimen, Benjamin Southern, Cedric El Frangi, Celine Angbeletchy, Chandler Davis, Chris Harmer, Chris Powell, Chuck Shepherd, Claudette Woodbridge, Craig Curtis, Cristiano Bernardi, Denis Sutyrin, Eileen Guo, Enrico Orsini, Eriko Gargiulo, George Fahmy, Giacomo Quadrelli, Guido Coli, Hamish McRae, Hanfei Zhang, Irune Ruiz Martinez, James Wynne, Jeannette J. Lucejko, John Donald Redmond, Kamran Bagheri, Karolina Gajda, Luciano Modica, Lusine Mkrtchyan, Manuel Herranz, Marco Pardini, Martin Gandy, Meera Mishan, Michelle Hopkins, Michelle Hopkins, Mike Seymour, Mohamed Shaban, Nikoloz Gorgodze, Nityanand Bolshette, Omer Masooq Qureshi, Orem Frien, Pandey Sushil, Pavel Belchev, Prashant Goel, Qin Yang, Ranjeeth Pasupathi, Riccardo Chiaverini, Richard McGowan, Richard Wydick, Ryszard Gawda, Sabine C. Gennai Schott, Sanjay Chikara, Saurabh Bhatia, Staph Bakali, Stuart Bett, Sue Fraser, Sue Odada, Tamang Asta Maya, Tarun Huria, Tommaso Wallwork, Tom Southern, Tushar Bansal, Valentina Prosperi, Veena Vishwa, Vi-Do Tran, Xiaojuan Mo, Yu Huan, Yung Guo Jiang, Zhou Shanshan

Thank you so much for allowing me to quote from your books and articles, from your emails to me, and from your conversations with me. This book would not have been possible without you.

Thank you to ION Trading and List Group for allowing me over the years to conduct interviews with staff and clients.

Thanks to Ann Marie Sabbath, Christalyn Brannen, Eileen Guo, and the publishers of Raymond Ng's book for allowing me to quote from their work.

A massive thanks to Anna Southern who cleansed this book of all my petty agendas, my pendant for inserting facts that are probably only of interest to me, and my frequent falls into stereotyping (despite the avowed aim of the book to avoid stereotypes). Thank you to Debbie DuFrene for editing this book.

A final thank you to the Plain English Campaign for doing such a fantastic job with cleaning up documents written in English.

Introduction

Is This Book For Me?

If you need to communicate in English with colleagues and clients who are not native speakers of English, then this book is for you.

This book is intended for people at all levels in the company hierarchy—from the receptionist, to the helpdesk, to sales staff, to top managers.

How Is This Book Organized?

Chapter 1 provides some background information into the dangers of stereotyping and introduces some key difficulties that non-natives have with the way we mother tongue speakers communicate in English.

Most business communication begins with an exchange of emails, which is the subject of Chapter 2.

Such email exchanges are often followed by an exchange of documentation. Chapter 3 thus focuses on the readability of your documents and suggests some strategies that will help your non-native counterparts to understand your writing.

Chapter 4 introduces the next stage of a business relationship—speaking. The idea is to make you aware of what elements of the way you speak may impede on successful communication.

Imagining that your business relationships are making progress, then the next step is conducting meetings and negotiations (Chapter 5) and giving presentations and demos (Chapter 6).

Chapter 7 introduces another key element of communication: the use of translation, translators and interpreters.

The last chapter in the book, Chapter 8, focuses on the social side of business communication.

Some key communication strategies overlap more than one chapter area so they are mentioned more than once, and are cross-referenced.

I Have Been Communicating in English For Years With Non-Native Speakers, and Very Effectively Too. SERIOUSLY, Why Do I Need This Book?

Vint Cerf is Chief Internet Evangelist at Google, and alongside Bob Kahn, is one of the fathers of the Internet. I have seen him present to non-natives and he absolutely has total command of what he is doing. Audiences love him. I asked him what his secret was. His reply:

> I have spent much of my career speaking publicly and privately with a broad range of audiences, from the ultra-technical to the general public. When speaking to and with people for whom English is not a native tongue, unsurprisingly, I have found it nearly universal that speaking more slowly and distinctly helps more than vocabulary changes, although I avoid special terms and acronyms when the audience is not expected to have command of the topic-specific argot.

Vint's approach is clearly a good one, and one that many native English speaking business people use. You yourself may use the same approach.

But speaking slowly and avoiding special terms is not enough. What possibly you may not know, is that ...

- It's not just a matter of avoiding overly technical words with a nontechnical audience. Counterintuitively, you generally need to choose the more sophisticated multisyllable Latinate words (*investigate*) over Anglo Saxon words (*look into*).
- If you have a nonstandard accent, there is a strong chance your audience will understand little of what you have said.

- If you check your interlocutor's understanding by asking questions such as *Are you following me? Does that make sense?* Most will say "yes," even if they have only been able to understand 10 percent of what you have said.

In addition, it is worth bearing in mind that:

- Spoken English is one of the most difficult languages to understand in the world; by contrast, written English is one of the easiest. Spoken English is not difficult to understand because it is complex (it actually has one of the simplest structures of any language), but because we tend to slur and swallow our words. Most speakers of other languages tend to enunciate words much more clearly.
- Even people who have lived and worked in another country for years and also speak the host country's language (and have thus experienced firsthand what it is like not to understand), often still speak too fast in English and use words that their listeners can't understand. Why? They are simply not aware that they are doing so; and no non-native has ever had the courage to tell them.
- The language you use is more important in terms of successful work relationships (at all levels in the company hierarchy) than knowing about any cultural differences between you and your counterparts.

Finally, to go back to Vint Cerf's quote, the word that stands out for me is "unsurprisingly." Be prepared in this book to be surprised by the number of other strategies you can use to improve your communication.

Rather than relying on an approach that apparently has always served you well, consider adding other tools to your kit of communication strategies. You should find you will get even better results.

In summary, you may think that you do not need this book. But you do!

Any More Reasons Why I Should Read This Book?

Most misunderstandings boil down to language. It's clearly not only a case of the words we use, but how we use them and how we say them. If this is true within our own language, when we communicate across cultures the problem becomes far more critical. However, because we know we are of different cultures, we tend to blame misunderstandings on differences in culture, ignoring the fact that we may simply have misinterpreted what the other person has said to us, or we may not have been clear in what we said to that person.

This book explains how to communicate in English with non-native speakers in a way that should minimize such misunderstandings.

For every native speaker of English, there are five non-native speakers. Although supposedly speaking the same language—English—the non-native speakers frequently cannot understand the native speakers, and vice versa. For non-native speakers, communicating with native speakers is a stressful and difficult process. Few native speakers make concessions, in terms of vocabulary used and speed of delivery, so that non-native speakers are left feeling bewildered, frustrated, humiliated, and with a slight (generally unconscious) feeling of inferiority that they have been unable to understand what has been said.

Several obstacles are a part of this confusion:

- Ignorance—the increasing decline in the number of Anglos speaking a foreign language, plus lack of knowledge about their own language, means that you may have little or no idea what it is like to not understand when someone is speaking to you in a language that is not your own.
- Arrogance, xenophobia, and cultural stereotypes. Books for travellers and business people on the culture they will be visiting usually present a very simplified version of reality. They give the author's personal but not necessarily represen-tative experiences, or according to the author's second-hand

and third-hand sources. This leads to sweeping generalizations of little or no value. Also, we often forget that non-natives probably know considerably more about our culture (through watching TV, movies, YouTube etc.) than we know about theirs.

- Misnomers about the language—readability indexes are supposed to identify words and sentences that do not conform to "plain English," but it is generally erudite English (i.e., Latin-based) that non-natives most readily understand.
- Cross-cultural communication—this supposedly scientific approach to studying the way people in different parts of the world communicate reduces the problem to "high" and "low" context societies, attitudes toward lateness, what gifts are acceptable, eating habits, how far you should stand away from your interlocutor and so on., These are generally marginal issues that obscure the true issue—language. Such studies also focus almost exclusively on what make cultures different rather than similar—this is clearly the wrong approach to setting up collaborations in whatever field.

This book provides a whole series of strategies for overcoming the obstacles listed above.

Who Else Might Benefit From Reading This Book?

Most of the strategies in this book are not exclusive to the business world and can also be applied in many other areas to avoid misunderstandings:

- Medicine—doctors misdiagnosing patients or not giving appropriate information; patients feeling helpless and frustrated.
- Science and research—attendees at international conferences cannot understand each other.
- Education and training—students cannot understand their teachers.

- Sport—players cannot understand their managers, and vice versa.
- Politics, law enforcement and the military—communication failure can even result in death.

If you are planning to live overseas in a non-Anglophone country, or simply planning a long trip abroad, you should be able to find a lot of useful information in this book.

CHAPTER 1

Getting Started

Eight things you didn't know you didn't know

- Lady Jane Grey, who was de facto Queen of England for nine days in 1553 before being beheaded in 1554, learned Greek, Latin, Spanish, and French when she was six, and Hebrew, Chaldee (an ancient Aramaic language), and Arabic before she was 17 (the age she was executed). She was also fluent in Italian.
- According to Aristides Konstantinides' book *The Greek words in the English Language*, there are 45,729 Greek words in English.
- When the United States moved toward independence in the 1770s, there was a drive to create a unique cultural identity. At the close of the American Revolution, some members of Congress proposed that the use of English be formally prohibited and be replaced by Hebrew, others proposed Greek.
- The English skills of a population apparently correlate with the economic performance of the country. According to EF (Education First), the top five best speakers of English are: (1) Netherlands, (2) Denmark, (3) Sweden, (4) Norway, and (5) Singapore.
- The top five IT companies in India spend around half a billion US dollars a year on education and training, including English language training.
- Many multinationals use English as the common corporate language—Airbus, Daimler-Chrysler, Fast Retailing, Nokia, Renault, Samsung, SAP, Technicolor, and Microsoft in Beijing.

- English words that Finnish has adapted include: *gangsteri*, *baari* (bar), *bestselleri*, *taksi* (taxi), *jatsi/jazz* (jazz), *televisio*, *filmi*. And Slovene: *vikend* (= weekend + little house where people spend the weekend), *sendvic* (sandwich), *tvid* (tweed), *inflacija* (inflation), *recepcija* (reception).
- In 2013, the European Court of Auditors produced a 66-page report entitled, "Misused English Words and Expressions in E.U. Publications." It noted that the form of English used in the European Union "differs from that of any recognized form of English" and "includes words that do not exist or are relatively unknown to native English speakers." Examples include: *actorness* (the quality of being an actor), *comitology* (committee procedure), *decommit* (cancel), *financial envelope* (budget), and *informatics* (IT).

1.1 What is the biggest obstacle to successful communication in English with non-native speakers?

We are.

Most of us in the Anglosphere don't speak another language. Let's take the UK as an example. A survey carried out by a travel website, Hotels. com, found that two thirds of Britons cannot say anything in a foreign language, with one fifth unsure of what "bonjour" means. However, 43 percent knew that *un cerveza per favor* means "a beer please" in Spanish. Nearly half of Britons aged between 16 and 24 have never used the foreign language they learned at school. This compares with the massive 94 percent of secondary students in Europe who are learning English, and who will then use it regularly in their work and social lives.

So what are the implications?

First, because we don't learn languages, we have really no idea of what it is like not to understand and not to be understood. We have never experienced this very humbling and often frustrating experience (nor have we experienced its rewards).

Second, we have no idea of how we sound to a non-native. We are not aware, for example, of these confusing habits:

- We swallow our words—either parts or even the entire word. For example, when you hear someone say *wanna go Wensdi* you understand that what they have really said is *do you want to go on Wednesday*. For a non-native this kind of automatic interpretation is difficult. Swallowing words and syllables is not a feature of many languages.
- Much of what we say is redundant (*ums, ahs,* unfinished sentences). This makes it difficult for non-natives who may not be sure whether an *um* is a word in itself or is the beginning or end of another word, or who may not understand that there may not be a logical step-by-step progression in what we are saying.
- We add to the confusion by using colloquial expressions.
- We may, unconsciously, use English as a powerful tool for dominating any communication in English with non-native speakers, particularly oral communication. We don't have to search for the right word to use, or mentally translate what someone else has just said. Talking is not an exhausting experience for us.

Unfortunately the result is that rather than feeling a sense of inferiority in our inability to speak another language, we actually feel the opposite. We just assume that everyone else should speak English and that everyone should understand us when we speak.

Conducting business internationally does NOT entail primarily learning about etiquette (whether to bow or not, whether to give someone a business card with one hand or two) or learning about other culture's approaches (power distance, high/low context communication, etc.). These are just the baseball equivalent of knowing which end of the bat to hold.

If you really want to learn how to *use* the bat effectively, infinitely more important are:

- Looking for similarities between you and your counterparts, rather being distracted by the differences.
- Speaking and writing in the clearest possible way; and listening carefully and patiently.

1.2 What stereotypes do other countries have of us and us of them? How reliable and useful are cross cultural guides?

If you are from the United States, which of the following concepts would you associate with yourself and your compatriots: friendliness, insincerity, capitalism, advanced society, paranoia, a model for the world, individualism, multiracial, gun-slinging?

In the Far East "individualism" and "multiracial" might stand out as key features given that many countries in that region are not multiracial in the melting pot sense of the United States and that group effort is prized above individualism. The British often find Americans to be insincere (superficial, overfriendly, too much personal information given too quickly), and most of Europe would comment on the American's occasional paranoia in how it conducts international relations.

But such stereotyping is often dangerous because it sets up expectations. These expectations may color the way we see and behave with members of other cultures.

Below are some extracts from two guides to the British written by two Americans. To what extent do they reflect your own opinion and experience of GB?

1. Uncomfortable with intense, continuous looks.
2. Discreet in their public behavior. Voices are never raised above a moderate volume, shouting is unheard of, and drawing any sort of attention to oneself is deemed a disgrace and causes immediate embarrassment.
3. Most have very bad teeth.
4. Loathsomeness of the French is exceeded only by the loathsomeness of the Germans.
5. Amused tolerance for drunken high jinks, even when practiced by flat-out drunks.
6. Pathological fear of being caught bragging.
7. Introducing yourself to a stranger at a party is considered rude.

The above points highlight various issues with guides to cross-cultural communication.

Some points (1 and 2), whether true or not, could apply to many different nations. Some (3 and 4) are only true of a tiny minority and cannot be generalized to a whole nation, others (5 and 6) may be true of many but it would be dangerous to extend them to every Brit you meet. Finally, some are simply wrong (7).

Here's another description about the supposed British love of a cup of tea.

> It is important to recognize that the answer to all of life's problems can be found after a nice cup of tea with a spot of milk. Be sure to offer a cup of tea and a biscuit (cookie) to the plumber, electrician or anyone who comes into your house. While tea may be drunk at any time of day, traditional tea time is between 3 p.m. and 5 p.m. and is often taken with finger sandwiches and cake. A cream tea will include scones, jam and clotted cream. High tea refers to an early evening meal.

The above text dates back to the early 1990s. It appeared on the site of Bennett and Associates, an international training and consulting firm who were bought out in 1996. The company claimed to be "specializing in the development of effective human resource strategies and interventions to increase the global success of our clients." Just how the above description, with its totally distorted picture of British life, would help anyone in their global success is unclear, especially given that it refers to a very limited sector of British society, that is, the economic elite who represent only about 6 percent of the population or the upper classes of 100 years ago.

Further dangers of making stereotypes are revealed by the following description. Which country do you think it is—would you consider going there?

- Most restaurants have bright fluorescent ceiling lights and a TV blaring.
- Black prostitutes line the roadsides.
- Men urinate in public.

- Pornography is on display at child height.
- There is religious, almost pagan, respect for the dead.

Or would you prefer this country?

- Children are adored and can even be picked up without fear by complete strangers.
- There are markets everywhere with fresh local produce.
- Educated adults can talk with authority about almost anything from history of art to philosophy to politics.
- Most people talk about their hometown with a great sense of pride and affection.
- People are generally always very clean, aided no doubt by regular use of the bidet.

If you read the first description you would never want to visit this country, yet almost 50 million tourists visit it each year. Exactly the same number visit the second country—why? Because they are both descriptions of Italy. The first is taken from a book entitled "Buying a house in Italy," the second are my own comments based on 30 years of living in Italy. Italians and most expats in Italy would certainly not see the first set as being in any way accurate, but may not agree with the second set either.

Finally, another danger with stereotyping is bracketing together a whole group of different nationalities. This is highlighted by Harry King author of *Spain, Your Guide to a New Life*:

[The Spanish] have some strange views about us [the British]. For a start, they seem to lump us all together whatever our nationality, and tend to regard all foreigners as northern Europeans who wear shorts, T-shirts and flip-flops, who spend days drinking beer and who lack education, manners and culture. Many Spaniards are also puzzled by the general British refusal to learn the language, which makes us stand out from other foreigners in our unwillingness to integrate and adapt to the Spanish way of life.

A typical pitfall of this lumping together: visitors to China who bow when being introduced to someone in the good intent to show respect to their host country. Bowing is, in fact, a Japanese custom not a Chinese one.

Both cross-cultural guides and cross-cultural consultants have their limitations. When writing a book on cross-cultural perspectives, the author wants to gain the interest of the readers and does this by highlighting the bizarre and exaggerating/distorting reality, just as one does when telling an anecdote at the dinner table. Also, much of the information given is second or third hand, that is, people who the author has met or details that the author has found from other sources (thus perpetuating any mistakes in those sources).

The moral of the story is not to read too much into descriptions in culture guides, websites, Facebook, Trip Advisor, and so on. Check out the experiences of colleagues and then go in with open eyes and really observe what is happening around you.

The limitation of cross-cultural consultants and guidebooks is that they home in on the differences, rather than what makes us similar. In addition, they tend to focus a lot on business etiquette, and not at all on language issues. Yet it is language issues that I believe are the main reason for cultural breakdowns and are the reason why I wrote this book.

That is not to say that there are no cultural differences, and that such differences do not have an impact on our dealings with non-natives. I teach PhD students of all nationalities and have encountered several differences:

1. The level of respect given to professors (and by analogy, managers) is much higher in some cultures, and this leads to considerably more formal relationships. In some cultures there is a much greater sense of hierarchy.
2. Facial expressions are much harder to read in some groups of nationalities. In fact, I would go as far as saying that facial expressions can be sometimes be impossible to read because often the face remains impassive. This is because in some societies at schools, the children are encouraged to listen passively to what they are told.

3. The number of questions and interactions with the professor tends to be much higher in students from the West. There is a greater sense that what the professor says can be questioned rather than taken as a given.

But what I have also noticed is that these differences tend to be accentuated in those students for whom my class is their first ever experience with lectures outside their home country. In fact, the more students have traveled and the longer they have been away from home, the less the three factors mentioned above come into play.

In the end, the three factors have far less impact on my relationship with my students than the way in which we communicate with each other in English. My experience in training employees in companies that have offices around the world has confirmed that the dynamics I have witnessed in my PhD classes match almost exactly the experiences business people have in the meeting room or videoconference room or dining room.

Having said all this, if you are going to embark on business in a market that is totally new to you, such as China or Japan, then there are good cross-cultural guides out there. Just ensure that you buy one that is for that specific country and that the author is either someone from that country or is someone who has lived there for a considerable amount of time. In any case, always begin your new business relationship with a totally open mind.

1.3 Who speaks English today?
A massive 1.75 billion people worldwide speak English at a useful level, according to an article in the *Harvard Business Review*.

So, as a native English speaker you may feel you can go anywhere and be understood. You may feel that even if you are not understood, the onus is on the other person to try and understand you, after all whose English is it anyway? But the fact is, as a native speaker, you are a minority. There are more people in China learning English than the total global community of native speakers (over a billion vs. around 400 million). Around 75 percent of the billion people who travel across borders every year move from one non-English speaking country to another non-English speaking country, yet communicate in English while they are there. So what is English's role today?

On Quora, the discussion forum, I asked the question:

> When you think of the English language, do you automatically associate it with the US/UK and so on; or does it now also have a life of its own no longer rooted in its cultural origins?

Among the replies, I received one extremely enthusiastic answer from Katja Kaila, a communications officer at the City of Helsinki (Finland). Katja is torn between her evident love of the language which she associates with English literature and its current role as the world's language, while also recognizing that it is the official language of many countries other than the UK and the United States:

> English is both this beautifully classic language that flexibly adjusts itself to all circumstances with elegance; and a lingua franca that's slightly annoying to resort to, in case other means of communication fail.

> When I think about English I also see my Nigerian-born colleague telling about his oil business, my Indian friend lecturing about literature in Kerala, and my Canadian friends in a small tent under the sky of a Caribbean island.

Katja, who speaks no fewer than six languages, concluded her answer very poetically by beautifully encapsulating the position of English today:

> English is a house built by natives all around the world, with all of us coming and going and leaving our muddy footprints on the floor and painting the walls with colors you perhaps wouldn't have chosen yourself; a strange combination of vagueness and precision, brokenness and charm.

I asked the same question on Facebook and directed it exclusively to non-native speakers. Respondents were pretty much split in their answers (55 vs. 45 percent). The fact that such a large number believe that English is not the exclusive possession of native speakers and that non-natives can create new nuances of grammar and coin new vocabulary, signals that we have as much a duty to learn "their" English as they do to learn "our" English.

> I would actually contend that the burden is really on us to learn their version of English and to communicate better to them when using our version.

1.4 What kind of English is spoken by non-native speakers?

During his conference years, Morris Schreiber (1927–1988), a theoretical mathematician and former professor at the Rockefeller University, travelled frequently around Europe. He quickly realized that there was "a common language for Poles, Hungarians, and Italians to communicate with each other. It's English; and I don't speak it." Schreiber set himself the task of speaking English in a way that would be unbaffling to non-native speakers.

Schreiber felt that essentially he was learning "English as a Second Language as a Second Language."

His philosophy was that we all need to learn how to speak another variety of English—not just our native variety, but the variety spoken by our non-native colleagues.

Schreiber's intuition over 50 years ago that he wasn't speaking the right kind of English, when outside the United States, is at the basis of Globish, a language based on a vocabulary of 1500 English words "invented" in the early 2000s by a retired IBM marketing executive, Jean-Paul Nerrière, who like Schreiber had been a very frequent participant at international conferences. In an article in the *New York Times*, Nerrière is quoted as saying:

> The language spoken worldwide, by 88 percent of mankind, is not exactly English. I don't think people who think this gives them an

edge are right because it's not useful if they cannot be understood by English speakers.

This concept of native speakers having "an edge" highlights that as a native speaker you should not use your command of English to your advantage. People will only want to work with you if they feel you are on an equal level—at least linguistically. Try to see English not as a language, but as a tool, a means of communication.

In an interview for my book *Business Vision* in 2001, Hamish McRae, one of Britain's most respected financial journalists and commentators, whose own book entitled *The World In 2020* had just been published, recounted that he hoped that in the future native English speakers would be:

> ... sensitive to this new role which English is taking on, and use their own language in such a way that it is easy for people who are non native speakers to understand them. Very often non native speakers speak better English than native speakers.

Although the issue of native English speakers not understanding (or not wishing to understand) the needs of their non-native counterparts, very little is being done about it by the English speakers themselves.

On the other hand, non-natives are spending billions of dollars a year learning and perfecting their English. They are also being taught strategies, such as the following by English language researcher Dr. Sue Fraser:

> If you fail to communicate successfully with a native speaker, do not immediately assume it is because of your English ability. Many native speakers are unaware that their spoken English is difficult to understand. This means that they often speak too fast, use inappropriate language (e.g., colloquial structures and expressions), and may also have a strong regional accent that you have probably never been exposed to before. The secret is not to be afraid or embarrassed, but to inform the native English speaker that you are unable to understand.

1.5 Why do some nationalities speak better English than others? What impact does their native language have on their ability to speak and write good English?

With some notable exceptions, the further you go east, the more a language is different from English. This means that western European languages tend to be more similar to English, than say Polish or Uzbek or Hindi or Chinese. Because, for instance, Armenian is so different from English, theoretically an Armenian would tend to make more mistakes than a Spaniard, though in reality it depends as much on the individual's talent for language learning. Also the intonation and speech patterns that they have in their own language will impact on the way they sound in English.

Most people when speaking in a foreign language tend to think in their own language and then mentally translate on the fly. Pavel Belchev, a Bulgarian who works for the European Commission, explains:

> All languages have a model of thinking that their speakers apply to their general way of perception. The language used determines consciousness. Once you are used to this model (almost always imposed by your mother tongue) it is very hard to switch to another one. When I speak English I still think in Bulgarian (or at least within the framework of my "Bulgarian model"). This is why I believe most of Bulgarians (or any non-English speaking person)—no matter how good their English is—would follow their Bulgarian model in the target language. This may result not only in mistakes but also in ambiguities. These ambiguities may either puzzle the reader or even result in understanding the essence of the sentence in a completely different way even though there were no grammatical or vocabulary mistakes made.

Another factor that influences the level of English of particular non-natives is the amount of exposure to English that they have. In Finland, the Netherlands, and Portugal, for instance, foreign language TV programs are always in the original language. The reason why so many people aged 50 and below understand spoken English so well (and in many cases also speak it so well) is that they have grown up hearing English on the television daily. On the other hand, countries such as Italy tend to dub everything into their own language. This means that Italian's understanding of spoken English will be quite low in comparison to those in Scandinavian countries, though being a loquacious people by nature, their spoken English may be reasonably fluent.

Speaking in another language can also cause frustration, as Meera Mithran, a life sciences researcher from India, told me:

> One thing I have experienced and felt is that even though I can speak fairly good English, I have never been able to fully express myself. For example the jokes you want to convey or if you want to talk your heart out, it is never the same as talking in my mother tongue (Hindi).

So when people are making the effort to speak to you in English, a language that they were not born with, it may help to bear these thoughts in mind:

- Their mistakes are highly likely due to the result of mental translation.
- Their listening skills may be related to whether their country watches TV in English, has access to YouTube, teaches English to kids from an early age, and so on.
- They are making a huge effort (with all the psychological frustrations that involves) to communicate with you, and are also doing you a massive favor by talking to you in your own language.

To learn how to speak more effectively to non-native listeners, see Chapter 3.

1.6 Why are there so many English words in other languages?

The fact that the native language that your client, your patient, your student, your acquaintance speaks is riddled with loanwords from English does not mean that their language is necessarily impoverished in any way. There is a tendency for English speakers to think their language, and hence their culture, is superior simply because they find English words used everywhere in foreign languages: in advertising, in the names of clothes, types of music, and so on.

The extent to which English has penetrated other languages is highlighted in this fictitious exchange between two Polish marketing managers.

	Poglish (Polish + English)	English translation
Piotr	Haj Jan, ho ar ja?	Hi, Jan, **how are you**?
Jan	Ajm fajn.	**I'm fine**.
Piotr	Jak **volumen**?	How are the sales **volumes**?
Jan	Brakuje mi paru **kejsw**.	I've still got a few **cases** to go.
Piotr	Musisz si **sfokusowa** na du ych **outletach**.	You must **focus** on big **outlets**.
Jan	Zrobi **budget**, ale musz **zapdejtowa** dane.	I will meet the **budget**, but I must **update** the data.
Piotr	Dobra, **sczekuj** wszystko i daj mi **feedback**.	**OK**, **check** everything and give me some **feedback**.

In reality, 60 percent of English comes from Latin (much via French). In the Polish exchange above, the words *fine, volume, focus, case, budget,* and the *date* in *update* all derive from Latin words. So it's really a case of words crossing borders and then coming home again for a few centuries before setting off on another journey.

English has in fact taken on a life of its own and is spawning new words. In Italy, people go *footing* rather than *jogging*, they get their kinky underwear from the *sexy shop*, and they *snob* people. The words they use may also change meaning or even grammatical form. Italians refer to "a jolly" meaning "a standby" (via the "jolly joker" in a pack of cards) and to women who are "in topless." They also change the pronunciation or stress and the spelling, so that a *pláyboy* becomes a *playbóy*, and *roast beef* becomes *rosbif.*

This appropriation of English is totally normal, and happens all the time in languages, including English itself. In fact, in the last 2000 years, the English language has done more than its fair share of appropriation of other languages, but we are often not aware of it. And when we are aware of it, historically we have tended to complain about it. Richard Mulcaster, the head of one of England's top schools, wrote in 1582 with regard to the impoverishment of the English language: *the latest terms which it boroweth daielie from foren tungs [foreign tongues], either of pure necessitie in new matters, or of mere brauerie [sheer ostentation], to garnish it self withall.*

1.7 What is listening to (the sound of) my English like for a non-native speaker?

When one language borrows a word from another language, it does so in many ways. One of the main ways, typically adopted when importing foreign words into English, is to use the same spelling but change the pronunciation. In English we use words like *bourgeois, brunette, chauffeur, chef,* and *depot,* probably without even thinking they are French, though we are more likely to recognize *déjà vu* as being French. However a French person would probably have difficulty in recognizing our pronunciation of "their" words.

Other languages, when adopting English words, will often change the spelling of the English word to make it conform to the sound system of their own language.

The words below are Russianized English words with a transliterated spelling from the Cyrillic alphabet into our Latin script. Can you work out what they mean?

klub
dress-kod
resepshn
autsorsing
auktsion
riteyl
franchayz
steyk-kholdery
fyuchers
kiberskvoting
tineydzhery
fayrvoly

The experience you go through in trying to work out the meaning of the words is similar to the experience many non-native speakers have when listening to you speaking in English. Some words they can recognize easily (*klub*—club, *dress-kod*—dress code), others sound familiar (*resepshn*—reception, *autsorsing*—outsourcing, *auktsion*—auction), and others they can take a guess at (*riteyl*—retail, *franchayz*—franchise). But some are virtually incomprehensible: *steyk-kholdery* (stakeholder), *fyuchers* (futures), *kiberskvoting* (cybersquatting), *tineydzhery* (teenagers), and *fayrvoly* (firewalls).

Being aware of how you sound to non-native speakers is one of the key steps to improving your communication.

To learn how to communicate orally to non-native listeners and with a clear pronunciation, see Chapters 3 and 6.

1.8 What difficulties might a non-native speaker have in trying to follow what i am saying?

The following is an extract from Molly's Monologue in James Joyce's *Ulysses* (Episode 18). To someone with a low to intermediate level of English, this is a little bit how you might sound to them.

> Fridays an unlucky day first I want to do the place up someway the dust grows in it I think while Im asleep then we can have music and cigarettes I can accompany him first I must clean the keys of the piano with milk whatll I wear shall I wear a white rose or those fairy cakes in Liptons I love the smell of a rich big shop at 7 1/2d a lb or the other ones with the cherries in them and the pinky sugar I Id a couple of lbs of those a nice plant for the middle of the table Id get that cheaper in wait wheres this I saw them not long ago I love flowers Id love to have the whole place swimming in roses God of heaven theres nothing like nature the wild mountains then the sea and the waves rushing then the beautiful country with the fields of oats and wheat and all kinds of things and all the fine cattle going about that would do your heart good to see rivers and lakes and flowers all sorts of shapes and smells and colours springing up even out of the ditches primroses and violets nature it is as for them saying theres no God I wouldnt give a snap of my two fingers for all their learning why dont they go and create something I often asked him atheists or whatever they call themselves ...

Obviously I am exaggerating somewhat by giving this as an example, but my point is that a non-native speaker:

- May have difficulty in understanding where one phrase ends and a new one begins (i.e., the same difficulty you will have just experienced in trying to decipher Joyce's stream of consciousness style above, which to many readers is just "noise").
- Will typically only be able to pick out certain words, and will not necessarily be able to judge whether these are key words or not, and how these words relate together to make an overall sense.
- May quickly find that effort of listening is simply too much and may thus switch off.

Of the final 24,048 words in Ulysses, there are only two full stops and one comma. Most readers have thus seriously struggled to decipher Joyce's tome. Your job, as explained in Chapter 3, Speaking and Listening, is to ensure that your listeners have no difficulty in digesting what you say, by putting yourself in their shoes and making it as easy as possible for them. This means planning what you are going to say before you say it, enunciating every word clearly, being aware of how your regional accent may be different from the standard English that your counterpart has learned at school, using relatively short sentences, choosing your words carefully (e.g., no slang, colloquialisms, buzzwords), minimizing redundancy, and not mumbling or swallowing your words.

1.9 How difficult is it for a non-native speaker to read a text in English?

The world has many alphabets. The one we use is based on Latin. But there are many others: Greek, Cyrillic (Russian and Slavic languages), Arabic, Urdu, Chinese, Japanese, and more than another 40 that are in use today. It requires a lot more effort for someone who uses another alphabet to read a text written in our alphabet.

Time yourself to see how long it takes you to read the following text—the first two letters of all words of more than four letters have been removed.

Consider that a non-native speaker, when reading any kind of text, might well make the same effort and take the same time as you will now.

> wever, the oblem for eakers of other nguages isn't mply a tter of ciphering tters and rds. You may ink at the der of the rds in an glish ntence is tally gical—bject rb ject—what uld be more vious? The fact is that the jority of the rld's nguages do not llow such an der, and many uld nsider eir der to be just as gical as ours

Too easy? Well try this:

> However, the problem for speakers of other languages isn't simply a matter of deciphering letters and words. You may think at the order of the words in an English sentence is totally logical - subject verb object - what could be more obvious? The fact is that the majority of the world's la nguages do not follow such an order, and many would consider their order to be just as logical as ours.

The text above is actually a flipped image of the complete version of the previous text, but in a different font. It is still in the English alphabet, although it may not look like it! It represents to some extent what it looks like when you have to decipher writing in a different script, particularly as you have to read it from right to left.

Here is the key:

> However, the problem for speakers of other languages isn't simply a matter of deciphering letters and words. You may think that the order of the words in an English sentence is totally logical—subject verb object—what could be more obvious? The fact is that the majority of the world's languages do not follow such an order, and many would consider their order to be just as logical as ours.

1.10 So how can I get relationships off to a good start if I am going to be working on a daily basis with people from another country?
A good strategy when working with people from a different culture is to have a meeting with the work group before a project begins or after a month or so of working with each other in which you discuss possible

issues, and work out how to deal with them. Questions that you might like to ask each other include:

- How much do you respect hierarchies at work?
- When addressing you via email, what conventions should we follow? How formal should we be?
- How will we able to know whether you have understood our English? Will you always tell us if you don't understand? Or should we try to check for understanding?
- Do we have different expectations in terms of decision making and taking the initiative?
- To what extent do you think both parties need to adapt to each other's ways? Do we need to agree on doing things in one standard way?
- What difficulties do you expect to encounter in your dealings with us? What difficulties have you had in the past? How can we avoid such difficulties in the future?

The idea is to predict the difficulties in advance and to work together to set up procedures to deal with them. Of course there are many things you will have to deal with as they come up. For example, many North Americans and Europeans find the level of formality of some of their Asian colleagues and partners too difficult to deal with. One of my European interviewees remarked of colleagues from Southern Asia:

> Even though we are at the same (low) level in the company hierarchy, I feel that I am being treated as if I am two steps above. They still call me "sir" after many months. This is particularly true for those Asian colleagues who are located in our offices in Asia, rather than those Asians located here in our offices in London. This unwarranted deference makes me feel awkward and presumably has a similar effect on my Asian colleagues—or is this just my sensation? What should my reaction be? Should I say not to call me "sir"? Might they be offended if I did this?

So the secret is to let the other person know that in the country or office where you are based, you adopt a much softer and friendlier approach to hierarchy. You can save their face by saying:

I appreciate your calling me "sir"; however, in our office the word "sir" tends not to be used, and if it were used it would be reserved for someone far higher in the hierarchy. I tend to feel that people work better if they feel they are on the same level and are all working toward the same goal—which is very much our case. So if it's OK with you, it would be great if we could just use first names to address each other, which I would imagine is pretty much in line with company policy.

In summary, when working with colleagues from a different culture, try to become aware of how business is conducted in that part of the world and how it may differ from the United States and UK in terms of the hierarchies (much steeper) and approachability to top management (more difficult). Here are a few guidelines:

1. Be respectful toward your colleagues as individuals or toward their culture in general (e.g., their religious or political situation).
2. Follow acceptable conventions when using salutations in emails (see Chapter 2).
3. Be sensitive about your colleagues. Respect any face-saving requirements (see Section 5.11), for example, don't show up a colleague in front of his/her team or boss, and understand that in a work environment there may be a reluctance to use the word "no."
4. Avoid bracketing people from the same country all together. For example, within Brazil or China or India there are many religions, cultures, and levels of wealth.

To learn more about respect and hierarchy, see Chapter 5.

Top Tips

- Be aware of the stereotyped views you may consciously or unconsciously have of other nationalities (including other English-speaking countries).
- Although some stereotypes may be true of big sectors of a population (e.g., Italians are fun-loving and appreciate good

food and wine), others may reflect experiences with a small and thus unrepresentative number of people (e.g., Italians are dishonest and corrupt).

- Stereotypes may only reflect certain aspects of life. In many cultures, much time is wasted on waiting: waiting in a line (probably the wrong one!) at a post office or government office, waiting to attract the attention of the shop assistant, waiting for friends to decide where to go out to eat tonight. But these waiting times don't necessarily transfer to the business or academic worlds which tend to adhere to international norms of acceptable waiting times.
- Be wary of what cross-cultural guides tell you. Any guide that is not specifically devoted to a single country and is not written by someone who is extremely familiar about that country is likely to make unreliable generalizations.
- By their very nature, cross-cultural guidebooks, particularly ones that cover vast geographical areas (Europe, the world), tend to focus on the differences, particularly the quirky but not necessarily typical ones. In reality, we share far more with other cultures than these guidebooks would have us believe.
- Don't view the massive import of English words into other languages as a sign of English's superiority—it is merely an example of the way words frequently change hands over the centuries. The English language has borrowed far more words than it has coined.
- Be conscious of the difficulties that the use of English can cause to non-native speakers.
- Before embarking on working relations with people of other nationalities and countries, set up some exploratory meetings together and come up with working methods that suit both parties.

CHAPTER 2

Email

Six things you didn't know you didn't know

- At the height of legal wrangles in the UK due to emails being sent to colleagues and bosses by semidrunk employees on their return to work from the pub for a Friday evening drink, software engineers came up with a program that could inform users whether they were drunk or not on the basis of pressure on the keyboard, the number of typos in the message, and the frequency of "inappropriate words." The problem of *drailing* (drunk emailing) was thus partially solved.
- The reason why some expressions in emails sound strange in the English of your non-native counterparts is that they are making a direct translation from their language. Here are some examples from German: *Sehrgeehrte/r Frau/Herr* = Very honored Mrs/Mr; *MitfreundlichenGrüßen* = with friendly greetings; *SchöneGrüße* = beautiful greetings; *SagenSieeinen-Gruß an Ihre Frau* = Say you a greeting to your wife; *Ichfreue-mich von Ihnenzuhören* = I feel pleasure for myself from you to hear (i.e., I look forward to hearing from you).
- First names that might appear to be feminine may in fact be masculine—Simone, Michele, and Andrea are all boys' names in Italy.
- Some nationalities go in heavily for titles, such as Herr Doktor Jones, and you may find yourselves being verbally addressed as Engineer, Lawyer, or Professor.
- There is only one form of "you" in English, compared to the three or four in Shakespeare's time and which still remain in most European languages. And this is nothing compared with Korean. A Korean speaker may have to choose between

six different verb suffixes (intimate, familiar, plain, polite, deferential, authoritative).

- A survey in London revealed that the work-related phrases that annoyed office workers most included "blue sky thinking" and "ideas shower." Andre Spicer author of *Shooting the shit: the role of bullshit in organisations*, attributes such kind of talk to the rise of meaningless work, or what anthropologist David Graeber has termed "bullshit jobs."

Note: Other aspects of writing are dealt with in Chapter 4.

2.1 What good email practices work well irrespective of what nationality I am dealing with?

Since 1971, when Ray Tomlinson sent the first email on the ARPARNET system (the precursor of the Internet), quadrillions of emails have been sent.

Here are some guidelines for drafting emails that pretty much work with anyone you write to, whether they be native or non-native speakers of English.

Subject Lines

- Compose the subject line from your recipient's perspective not your own.
- Be specific, never vague.
- Consider using a two-part subject line.
- Ensure that your subject line is not spam friendly.
- If possible, make it clear if your mail only requires very limited effort on the part of the recipient.

First Contact

- Explain where you got your contact's details from.
- Give details about who you are; or remind your recipient who you are, where you met, how you have had previous contact. Paint a clear picture of who you are for your recipient.
- Make your request/s clear.

- Ensure that the info appended after your "signature" contains everything that your recipient may need to know (contact details, etc.).
- Avoid PSs and anything under your "signature"—they simply may not be read.

Attachments

- Make it clear that a document is attached by using the word *attached* or *attachment*. If you simply say *Here is ... Hope you find this useful.* Your recipient may not even realize that you have attached a doc.
- Tell your recipients what feedback or action you expect them to take in relation to the attachment.
- If you are forwarding a doc, explain in the subject line or in the first line of your email why you think the recipient might benefit from reading the doc.

Requests

- Consider whether it might be wiser just to make one request rather than several. When presented with three or four requests, many recipients will just respond to the one that is quickest to deal with and ignore the others.
- Lay out your request clearly: use short sentences and plenty of white space—avoid blocks of text.
- Give recipients all the information they need to carry out the request.
- For multiple requests, include a mini summary at the end of the email.
- Give deadlines.
- Motivate your recipients to reply by empathizing with their situation and showing them respect.

Main Body of Your email

- Be sensitive to the recipient's point of view.
- Organize the information in your email in the most logical order, and only include what is necessary.

- Bear in mind that long emails will be scrolled.
- Prefer clarity over conciseness.
- Include a summary and action points that you want the recipient to take.

2.2 What's in a name? How can I tell whether someone who has written to me the first time is male or female?
Often it is impossible. But this doesn't just apply to foreign names. For example, are Saxon Quinn, Robin James, or Ainsley Wayne male or female? Saxon sounds pretty masculine, but many of the Saxons I found on the Web are female.

When you get an email for the first time from a new contact, typically the name in your inbox will appear as, for example, *John Doe*. Then in a chain of emails you will just see *John* in the inbox. This is not a universal practice.

For example, this is how an online article referred to the world's youngest computer wiz:

> After passing the Microsoft Certified Professional test, when she was just eight years old, young M. Lavinashree has now become the world's youngest Red Hat Certified Engineer. M. Lavinashree was born in rural Tamil Nadu, India, but her parents noticed her incredible mind, when she was just a baby.

Lavinashree is in fact the girl's first name.

I think both sides of the equation (non-Indian and Indian) need to be aware of the potential confusion here. If you are writing to someone of another nationality and your name is not clear, then you can explain this in your signature. So if you are Indian in the body of your email you could write:

> Dear Adrian,
>
> My name is M. Lavinashree and I am a project manager at ... Just to avoid confusion, my first name is Lavinashree (I am female)

and my family name is Mahavira. I know that Adrian is both a male and female name, so perhaps you could tell me what it is in your case. So ....

You can also consider indicating your sex in your signature so: M. Lavinashree (Ms), Adrian Wallwork (Mr). Why should you care about the gender of the person you are writing to? I personally find it helps to picture the person I am writing to. But more importantly, if I phone my project manager and I am expecting to hear a man's voice and I hear a woman's, then I might be confused (even more so if the call is a video call via Skype).

In summary

- In your own email signature make it clear whether you are male or female—for example, Jo Smith (Ms). If you don't want to use Mr. and Ms. in your signature, at least make it clear in your email that Jo can be a female name as well as a male name.
- Don't assume that the rest of the world uses our *given name + family name* formula. For example, in the Chinese name Tao Pei Lin, Tao is the surname and Pei Lin is the given name.
- It helps if you can become aware of the email practices of any country that your company or institute may be dealing with. For example, if you are writing to Chinese people, then you might address them as "Respectful" or "Honorable" followed by their name. "Dear" is not used as much in mainland Chinese culture as in the Anglosphere because it involves intimacy (to mainland Chinese people "dear" sounds like "darling" or "sweetie" or "honey"). In mainland China *dear* is generally used between close female friends and between lovers.

2.3 Does the way people write emails in English vary much from country to country?

My company gets emails from all over the world. We have noticed that the length and the level of formality and politeness of the email is often more in relation to the individual and how familiar they are with the concise and more informal US style of writing mails than whether they are Italian, Iranian, Japanese, and so on.

Instead what really distinguishes one nationality from another is not really the way they write English (short vs. verbose, very formal vs. informal) but in their salutations. The English of 100 years or more ago was full of expressions such as *Most honorable sir* and *Your faithful and affectionate Servant*, that is, very formal phrases which to some extent Indian English has inherited and which other Englishes have dispensed with in favor of simple expressions such as *Dear X* and *Best regards*. Some examples from emails I have received from readers and clients around the world are as follows.

INITIAL SALUTATION	FINAL SALUTATION
Hi sir, (Philippines) Dear sir Wallwork (Vietnam) I am very delighted and honored to be able to contact you. (China)	Thank you in advance for your concern. (Korea) Thanks a world in advance for your kind prompt reply.(Iran) I remain most respectfully yours. (India)

2.4 How can I cement a good relationship with my recipient?

Different nationalities have different expectations as to how an email should look and sound.

Here is an exchange between Luigi a non-native speaker and his colleague *Bill* (a native speaker) who has inserted his replies into Luigi's previous message.

Dear Bill
Hope all is well with you.
Re the meeting, I think it would be best if I was just there anonymously.
Sure, no problem
So it will be in a room on the second floor in P3, right?
Just booked Room 2.02
Best regards
Luigi

Looks like a normal exchange doesn't it? However, Luigi finds Bill's style aggressive, even though he knows that it is not intended to be. Luigi, like some (but certainly not all) Italians, likes emails to begin and end with some kind of salutation, and prefers to be a little indirect. So often it is a matter of personal style, rather than any cultural differences. Verma, an Indian colleague of Luigi's, complains that Luigi's emails are too long and in chains of emails finds it difficult to identify who wrote what.

There is no right way to cement a good relationship, but it might be a good idea to take your lead from the other person. If that person seems to use salutations at the beginning and end, and perhaps ask you a question about your weekend, the weather, the football results, and so on, then take those extra five seconds to do the same.

I am not suggesting that you mirror your counterparts' emailing technique completely, just their salutation style and whether they seem to adopt full sentences (rather than a telegram style) when inserting their replies. However if someone writes irritatingly long and unstructured emails, then you could politely point this out by saying something like:

> I just wanted to say that we are extremely busy at the moment. So it would be really helpful if you kept your emails short, as unfortunately we don't have that much time to read them. Thank you so much.

My own emails tend to be short, with a series of short often numbered or bulleted sentences, which to some recipients may sound rather abrupt or even rude. The secret is that when you are going to have a new work relationship with someone, it is worth taking the time to explain any idiosyncrasies in your style so that no one takes offence. I typically explain that experience has taught me that short sentences (in a series of bullets) tend to be clearer for the reader, who is thus more likely to reply with the information I need.

Cementing a good relationship depends above all on writing clearly so that your recipient has no problem understanding exactly what you mean. Non-natives have to make far more effort than we do when reading and deciphering an email written in English. So if they can understand your email, not only will you have enabled them to act on your request/

instructions, but you will also have done them an enormous favor as they won't have to write back to you for explanations.

Eight Tips for Maintaining Good Relationships via email

1. Choose a suitable level of formality—in your initial dealings with people, opt for a more formal approach. Then become more informal as the relationship develops.
2. Ensure you spell the person's name correctly.
3. Never adopt a tone that is condescending, patronizing, or too authoritative.
4. If this is your first email to someone, show it to a colleague who has had regularly dealings with the company, nationality, or person you are writing to. Your colleague should be able to spot any inappropriateness in your writing and in your tone.
5. When sending reminders, don't make any accusations without knowing the full facts. It could be that your counterpart has not replied because of illness, electrical power failure, or simply more urgent work than yours. Don't jump to the worst conclusion. Be diplomatic.
6. When you need to criticize someone, maintain a mental picture of your counterpart being someone like you—smart, reliable, conscientious—rather than an incompetent fool.
7. When saying anything that could be construed as a criticism, structure your email so that the focus is not only on the criticism. Use the first words to set a positive tone, be diplomatic, and make detailed comments rather than unspecific observations. Use shorter sentences when you have something good to say, and use longer sentences for the "bad" news. Conclude your report by saying something positive.
8. Reread everything before you hit the "send" button. Check for anything that could be interpreted as being overly negative or unwarranted, or that is not 100 percent clear. Remember that people read emails extremely quickly and often don't read every word/sentence/paragraph. So your key message must be extremely clear.

2.5 What can I do to resolve any misunderstandings that have arisen through email communication?

Communication is always two-way—so both parties generally have equal responsibility. Don't jump to any conclusions based on stereotypes of a particular nation or race. Be sensitive to the fact that they are communicating with you in your language, not theirs—therefore to some extent the onus is on you to be patient and understanding.

A misunderstanding may arise via email because your non-native counterparts may:

- Be unable to distinguish between formal and informal English, or between rude and polite English forms, and thus come across to you as having an inappropriate tone.
- Be too embarrassed to admit that they hadn't understood something.
- Not have realized that a request was being made and/or that it was being made specifically to them.
- Not even have received your message.

If the problem is not the tone or content of the message, but the fact that action has not been taken or was not carried out correctly, then the best solution is to admit there is a problem, and get them to suggest solutions as well as suggesting possible solutions yourself.

Many misunderstandings result simply from the fact that most people do not write emails very carefully. If your instructions are not totally clear, then the recipients will tend to interpret them in the way that requires the least amount of action on their part or that matches what their previous experience seems to dictate they should do. For example, I emailed a friend who is a highly experienced business negotiator to "look through" the chapter on meetings and negotiations in this book. I was simply expecting her to write a few comments to confirm whether what I had written about negotiations was accurate and reflected her experience. She is used to editing and double checking business contracts and reports in her company—so rather than commenting on my chapter, she simply proofread it—with no input at all about her experience with negotiations.

Basically she was doing what she would have done with any document anyone emailed her—I should have been much more specific in my instructions. I thus ended up wasting her time and mine.

Misunderstandings also arise because the recipient simply didn't read what you had written—perhaps your key instruction was written at the end of the email and he/she only scanned the beginning of the mail. Or maybe you had given a series of requests, and your recipient answered the request that was easiest to answer and ignored (or didn't even read) the others.

So before you launch into a criticism of your recipient, it always pays to check that what you wrote was actually clear. In any case, always be constructive and polite.

And of course, there can be misunderstandings even among native speakers. An email I received from my American editor on the first draft of this book said it was *quite informative* and *quite comprehensive*. I was not happy. For a British person like me, the word *quite* is a put down. If I say your work is *quite good*, it means anything from "reasonable" to "barely reaching the required standard"—see Section 3.10 for more on interpreting British modes of giving criticisms. I then discovered from the Macmillan Dictionary blog that *quite* is the "trickiest word in American" and I was relieved to find out that it actually meant *very*!

So, again, before you curse your counterpart, double check whether there might be another interpretation to what you think you have read. Here is the beginning of the email I received:

> I have enjoyed reading your manuscript and found it to be quite informative. It is quite comprehensive, given the word count, which is well within BEP guidelines. I especially like the chapter introductions which focus on pivotal facts for the topics covered. I also like the question/answer format used throughout and the numerous inclusions of comments and viewpoints from various cultural perspectives.

In fact, apart from the word *quite*, the rest of the email seems to have a very positive tone, which should have been an immediate sign to me that my initial impression was wrong. But my British eyes had only zoomed in on *quite* and had thus blurred my vision as to the rest of the content.

When you receive an email that for whatever reason doesn't match your expectations, you might find one or more of the following strategies useful:

- Reread it to see if your first impression is confirmed.
- Leave it for a while, and come back to it with fresh eyes, or get someone else to read it.
- Check to see whether the offending word or phrase might possibly have another meaning in the variety of English that your interlocutor speaks.
- If the writer is a non-native, consider that what you have read may not have been what the writer intended and could just be the result of a poor translation.
- If you are convinced that something is awry, check with the writer that your impression is correct, but without an accusatory tone.

2.6 How concise should I be? what kind of language should I use?
Ricardo Semler, the maverick CEO of Semco SA in Brazil, once wrote that:

The longer the message, the greater the chance of misinterpretation.

However, there are also dangers of being too concise. For you just writing the word *Thoughts?* at the end of an email may be enough to invite comments from the recipient. But a non-native speaker may have no idea what you mean.

A sentence such as:

Wanted to get your feedback in the meantime.

May be confusing because there is no subject to the verb *wanted.*

Why should a non-native be expected to know what CW stands for in the following email?

I am planning to be in Havana in CW 38. Maybe this could be an opportunity to get to know each other.

So until you are sure that your recipient's level of English is very high, then opt for full versions:

Thoughts = What are your thoughts on this?
Wanted = I wanted ...
CW 38 = In the week beginning July 10. [CW—calendar week]

Also, try to develop a sense of awareness of when you might be using slang or idiomatic expressions (e.g., *it ticks all the boxes*). A phrase made up of words that individually mean one thing but put together mean a totally different thing may cause confusion for your recipients.

Leaving aside the technical jargon, can you identify the parts of the following mail that a non-native might have difficulty in understanding?

I seem to recall there was a setting for issues to go to a Jira based, built-in, database, rather than the SQL DB backend. Was this the problem? If this was a one-off, then worry not. Other than that perhaps I ought to amend my pre-commit scripts to catch this condition. So far I'm pretty much relying on the Jira integration to do what it says on the tin.

The problem is that the writer is expressing himself in a stream of consciousness way, without going back to edit his thoughts. In this case, being more concise or precise would have helped. For a non-native, the difficult expressions in the preceding email would be *one-off, worry not, pretty much, do what it says on the tin*.

Eleven Phrases to Avoid in emails to Non-natives

at the end of the day I think

bring you up to speed

have had my back up against the wall

how's tricks?

just a heads up on

keep me in the loop

let's touch base on Friday

push the envelope

thinking outside the box

we're all singing from the same hymn sheet

whose brainchild was this?

Finally, ensure that your whole email isn't just a series of colloquialisms. This email was received by one of my clients—she was totally mystified by it.

So far not a flutter from my customers ... fingers crossed the problem has gone down the plug hole!

2.7 How can I know if I am using the right kind of vocabulary?

It will help an email relationship considerably if you can sensitize yourself to the difficulties that your readers might have in terms of understanding the type of words you use in your emails.

It may seem logical to write short simple words. However, this is no guarantee that your counterpart will understand. In fact, when writing to non-natives, words that we might consider to be more complex may actually be more understandable for them. The reason is that the English language has two main roots: languages that were once spoken in north Germany, Denmark, Sweden (for the sake of simplicity let's call this the Anglo-Saxon side of English vocabulary), and Latin. Non-natives of any language tend to find Latin words easier to understand, as such words will either be closer to their own language (e.g., Spanish and French speakers) or will simply be what they have encountered in their English language textbooks at school.

Below is a sample of Latinate words and their Anglo-Saxon equivalents (see also Section 4.3):

alleviate (ease), approximately (roughly), ascertain (find out), consequently (so), encounter (meet), enquire (ask), entire (whole), necessitate (need), nocturnal (nightly), observe (watch), occupation (livelihood), pardon (forgive), prior (beforehand), prioritize (rank), profession (job), prohibit (forbid), projection (outlook), response (answer), salary (wage), verify (check)

Non-natives find some kinds of verbs that are made up of two or three words (known as phrasal verbs) to be particularly difficult. So you might find your recipients understand you better if you write, for example, *precede* rather than "go before," *revise* or *check* rather than "go through," or *accompany* rather than "go with."

2.8 What else can I do to ensure that my emails are understood?

Below are some more tips to help your readers understand your email messages.

Double Check for Typos

Emails are often sent in a hurry without being reread, so typos often appear. Typical typos include inverted letters such as *from/form, use/sue, filed/field, through/trough* or because you have written *their* instead of *there* or *they're*. A native speaker will immediately (and often unconsciously) understand that what they are reading is a typo—a non-native doesn't have this facility and may waste much time trying to figure out a meaning. So double check your mails before sending them—a spell check is not enough (it won't spot that you wrote *asses* instead of *assess, addiction* rather than *addition*, or *spare prats* rather than *spare parts*).

Double Check for Missing Words, Particularly a Missing "Not"

It is very easy to write: *Just to let you know that I am coming to the meeting,* when in fact you meant *I am not coming*. This kind of oversight will even confuse your native-speaking colleagues. If you read your email aloud you are more likely to spot the mistake.

Don't Use Abbreviations, Unless they are Standard Business Ones

How do you think your reader might react if you wrote the following?

*If you'd like to pop in just for a short chat on Fri aft that would be
brill. Tata, Phil*

Instead spell out the full forms: *Friday, afternoon, brilliant.* Some expressions, such as *tata* (British colloquial English for *bye bye*) might even be
confusing for other native speakers.

Consider Providing Explanations and Examples of Particular Words You've Used

Sometimes you may want to use a particular word because you feel it is
the most appropriate or because it is commonly used in your workplace.
However, if you also feel that it might be misunderstood, consider putting a synonym in brackets or provide an example of what you mean.
Here's an example, imagining that you think your reader may not understand the word *punchy*:

> We need to make the content more punchy (i.e., more dynamic).
> We need to make the content more punchy (e.g., we could use
> words such as *boost* ....).

Structure Your Email So that Your Requests Stand Out Clearly

Many emails are not acted upon appropriately simply because the recipient didn't even notice the request/instruction because of where it was
located in the email, for example, in the middle of a long paragraph or at
the end of the email.

2.9 What other ways are there to improve email communication with non-native speaking colleagues?

I conducted a survey for one of my clients to help them improve their
communication with their offices in India. I asked some of my client's
staff to write down questions that they would like answered by their
Indian counterparts.

On the next two pages are some of the questions (in italics). These were
then answered by several Indian colleagues. Clearly the answers given
are subjective, and may vary from individual to individual (and certainly
from one geographical region to another).

When addressing our colleagues in India via email, what conventions should we follow? How formal should we be?

In a work environment, casual and friendly emails are treated with minimal priority. It also depends on how well you know the individual and how long you've worked with him/her. With a completely new contact, it's best to be very formal and polite.

How can we indicate that we need a quick answer?

Use words like "Important," "Urgent" would help. Specify a deadline. To trigger a prompt response, be formal and put their manager in cc.

How can we encourage our colleagues in India to take the initiative?

Increase their confidence level by giving them responsibility for a particular task, rather than simply asking them to do the task. From the very beginning, involve them in discussions at work/meetings relevant to their field/scope of work. Invite them to informal social events/ coffee breaks with colleagues.

When we ask you about a reasonably simple problem, are you more likely to refer to a superior before replying to us, or will you write back directly?

This will depend on how clearly an employee's role has been defined for him/her. For example, if an employee is asked explicitly to collaborate with a colleague on a particular task, he/she will answer the questions directly instead of referring to the superior. Again much depends on their level of confidence.

If we ask you to fix a problem, it seems that you only fix that one problem, without fixing related problems that clearly need fixing too.

The employee may be unsure about whether he/she should do something or not—again it is a problem of lacking confidence. You may have noticed that this problem doesn't happen with the senior employees.

Why don't you tell us when you don't understand something? Why don't you ask more questions?

India is a huge nation with various religions and cultures. The employees' approach to their work may also depend on their geographical and cultural background. If an individual hails from not very well-to-do families whose parents have not worked in the corporate world, then there is always a hesitation to show that he/she is unsure of something. While it is a gross generalization, it can be said that Indians from the north tend to be more extrovert, while those from the south are more introvert and may ask fewer questions or try to understand the question by themselves before coming back with more questions. Another possible explanation is that the English accent of south Indians is very different from rest of India, so they may be embarrassed to show that they have not understood which, if they were speaking, would reveal their (poorer) English accent.

As a result of this survey, which was conducted both ways (i.e., the Indians also had their own list of questions), relationships between the various offices improved immensely. You could consider conducting a similar "survey" if you are part of a business with international partners.

Depending on your position with respect to your recipients, you can also give them instructions. The following email was written by a university secretary in the United States whose job is to deal with applications by foreign students. This is her first email to the student, but as you will notice, experience has taught her that setting some "ground rules" helps to oil the communication:

> I am the graduate secretary here (I coordinate your application material for review by the Grad Studies committee and interface with the Faculty of Graduate Studies (Admissions)). I think things are slightly less formal here than in India, so you can address me by my first name. During the application process, we will probably email back and forth quite a bit, so don't worry if my or your emails are short and direct!

2.10 How important is punctuation?

Very! You can totally confuse your readers if you misuse or fail to use punctuation. If you need convincing of how punctuation can completely transform a message, then read this classic example:

> Dear John
> I want a man who knows what love is all about. You are generous, kind, thoughtful. People who are not like you admit to being useless and inferior. You have ruined me for other men. I yearn for you. I have no feelings whatsoever when we're apart. I can be forever happy—will you let me be yours?
> Jane
>
> —
>
> Dear John
> I want a man who knows what love is. All about you are generous, kind, thoughtful people, who are not like you. Admit to being useless and inferior. You have ruined me. For other men, I yearn. For you, I have no feelings whatsoever. When we're apart, I can be forever happy. Will you let me be?
> Yours,
> Jane

Use of punctuation varies from country to country. In English, we tend to use punctuation to help our readers understand better the structure of a sentence. So if you've written any long sentences, check whether an extra comma might not make it more immediately comprehensible.

The use of capital letters in many languages doesn't follow the same rules as in English. This means that you might receive rather strange looking emails and letters beginning, for example, like this:

> *Dear Mrs Jones,*
> *we thank You for Your interest in our company ...*

In fact, capital letters are often used in other languages to denote the polite form of "you," and the first line of their email may start with a lower case letter.

For more on punctuation, see Section 4.8.

Top Tips

- Don't be as concise as you would be with a native English speaker. Spell things out clearly, and write a short summary at the end of a long mail.
- Opt for reasonably short sentences; make it clear when you are making a request, and space ideas and requests out with white space.
- Learn how to deal with names. Tao Pei Lin—Gender? First name? Family name?
- Don't jump to a negative conclusion about people merely based on errors in their emails.
- Don't naturally assume that apparently blunt sounding expressions are intended to be rude; it's far more likely that the non-native writer was unable to express themselves in the way intended.
- Don't judge a non-native speaker by a few spelling mistakes, typos, or strange-sounding salutations.
- Be neutral in an email. You don't know who will read it, what mood they will be in, who it will be forwarded to, how it will be interpreted, and so on. Write in a neutral, cautious way.
- Nothing is universal. Some people write in a complicated way, others of the same nationality/age/sex/position opt for a simpler way. So don't just assume that someone is behaving or writing in a particular way because he/she is of a certain nationality.
- Ensure any requests and instructions in your emails are clear. If there is misunderstanding, before accusing your counterpart, go back and check whether the confusion arose because your email was open to interpretation or was badly constructed.

CHAPTER 3

Speaking and Listening

Six things you didn't know you didn't know

- The most languages ever learned by one person is supposedly 50 or more, but that leaves another 6,950 languages that the individual doesn't know.
- When Scottish singer Susan Boyle was interviewed on *The Oprah Winfrey Show*, her remarks were subtitled at the bottom of the screen. And when Apple launched its speech interpretation and recognition interface (Siri), it had problems recognizing and interpreting some Scottish accents.
- Simon Cowell, the executive producer of the X Factor, recommends that if British neo-stars are going to break into the US market, they should enroll in elocution lessons. According to Stuart Levine, a TV writer for Variety: "The English accent, especially with those dialects, can be really tough to understand."
- As late as 1914, British army regiments had to be based regionally: for example, a Cockney (a native to London) could neither understand a Glaswegian, nor a Cornishman (a native of Cornwall) understand a Geordie (Newcastle). So speakers from the same geographical area had to be grouped into the same regiment.
- The lyrics of many modern songwriters are spectacularly difficult to understand not only for non-native speakers, but also for us natives, as highlighted by the need for websites such as www.amiright.com.
- English has 16 spellings for the sound *sh: anxious, chic, conscious, crucial, fuchsia, issue, mansion, nation, nauseous, ocean, pshaw, schist, sentient, shoe, sugar, suspicion.*

3.1 How should I address someone?

When addressing someone for the first time, remember that your interlocutor is likely to be a little nervous given that they have to speak in your language rather than theirs. The trick is to put them at ease by speaking slowly and enunciating your words very clearly. You could say: *Good morning. My name is John Doe.*

They may already know your name. But if they don't, repeat it again slowly. So: *My name is John Doe. John Doe.*

You can also add: *I am very pleased to meet you.*

Some cross cultural gurus recommend learning some greetings in the language of your counterpart, i.e. to show respect. For example, when two Koreans meet, they say the equivalent of: *I've met you, so I'm pleased* or *I am seeing you for the first time.*

This does not mean that you should use their English version. You can try pronouncing the greeting in Korean if you wish, but it may be very difficult to pronounce correctly and your interlocutor may not be clear what exactly you have said.

But there is nothing to stop you from using a greeting in their language when writing an email to them—just ensure that the spelling is correct.

3.2 When talking to a non-native, I typically adopt a kind of Pidgin English. Is this a good approach?

In the second decade of the 17th century, the first African slaves were brought from West Africa to Virginia to work on the tobacco plantations. The slaves were deliberately organized into groups with different language backgrounds, thereby preventing easy communication and thus avoiding rebellion. On board the slave ships, the Africans developed a pidgin (i.e., a simplified form of language) with the sailors—many of whom spoke English. Once in the United States or Caribbean, this pidgin English continued to be the means of communication between the slaves and their owners, and then became the basis of the language of the second and later generations.

Pidgin varieties thus exist in their own right, almost as separate languages. But the concept that most of us have of "pidgin" is a simplistic and distorted version of the original language, which is supposedly used by someone with little or no command of the language.

So the question is: is it appropriate to use a very simplified form of English in one's dealings with foreign counterparts?

The answer is "no." But why?

A contact of mine, who once worked with the Vancouver Police Department and the Royal Canadian Mounted Police on a program training young Japanese police officers, wrote to me saying:

> It was glaringly obvious that the Canadian police, in spite of working in a multi-ethnic, multi-lingual society, had no idea of how to ameliorate their English to make it more comprehensible to the Japanese constables. The Canadian constables were incapable of identifying what in their speech patterns made their English hard to understand for the Japanese.

> Even in lectures about "tactical communication," where the object was to communicate the officer's intention clearly (and loudly), as in "do NOT move," the Japanese were often at a loss as to what was being said. The Canadians usually simply increased the volume of their speech, or began to use a kind of foreign-talk, viz. "You, YOU DROP KNIFE? You, YOU NO RUN."

This "foreign talk" approach does not work well. In fact, instead of making what you are saying easier to understand, you actually make it more difficult. This is because this pidgin style does not match the English that your interlocutor will be used to hearing, nor does it follow the grammatical rules that they are likely to have learned. The pidgin style is also offensive, as you are basically treating your interlocutor like an inferior.

So avoid:

- Deleting words such as *a* and *the* from your speech and only using the infinitive form of verbs (e.g., *We go now bar, you come too? You no understand?*);
- Finishing a word or sentence for your counterpart;
- Increasing the volume of your voice when your counterpart appears not to understand;
- Imitating their English accent thinking that it might make your English more understandable for a non-native.

The rest of this chapter outlines a series of approaches that, on the other hand, do work.

3.3 How does a native speaker of English sound to a non-native? What do I need to know about speaking more clearly?

The following three waves reproduce the sound made by three people saying the five-word sentence *I want to go now*.

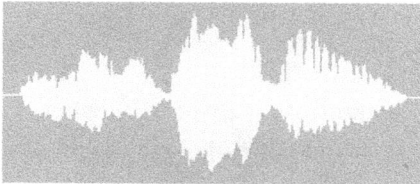

Wave 1 Speaker: A 28-year-old from London speaking at normal speed. Note how there are essentially 3 blocks (*wanna*, *go*, *now*), although 5 words are spoken.

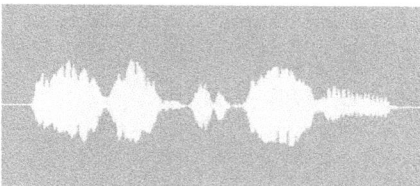

Wave 2 Speaker: A native English-speaking elocutionist, enunciating each word slowly. The 5 words are much more clearly separated.

Wave 3 Speaker: A 28-year-old Italian speaking in English at a normal speed. Note how the pattern is very similar to Wave 2. Non-natives often tend to pronounce each word as if it had equal importance.

Ideally, a non-native would like to hear English spoken as in Wave 2, where the words are said not only more distinctly than in Wave 1, but also reflect the way a non-native would speak (Wave 3), thus making the sentence much more familiar-sounding and recognizable.

The three blocks of Wave 1 highlight how in English we stress certain words—*wanna, go, now*—whilst the others (*I, to*) get almost swallowed completely. As native speakers, we are able to identify the important words in a spoken sentence simply from the stress given to them.

Non-native speakers don't have this ability. For them each sound that they hear potentially has the same importance. This means that they cannot filter out the noise, and they cannot separate the bands of sounds—for them the three bands in Wave 1 are all just one long blurred sound.

So you can massively help your listeners if you learn to enunciate each word clearly. This does not mean that you have to give each word equal stress and produce a robotic monotone. It simply means that you speak more slowly, and use your mouth and tongue to make the sounds of the words easily perceptible. This "eating" or "swallowing" of words by native speakers can really distort the sound of some everyday words. Try saying these words aloud and you will note that certain letters disappear: *Wednesday, business, medicine, difference, comfortable, interesting, vegetable.* You can help non-natives by saying such words a little slower than you normally might.

3.4 I have quite a strong regional accent. What can I do to help non-natives really understand my spoken English?

Sometimes we find other native English speakers difficult to understand. John Redmond from Canada recalls a period spent in Scotland:

> The only person I understood during my week's visit to Glasgow, was the Sikh taxi driver who took me to the airport!

Timothy Mitchell, from Texas, found working in a London company often very difficult, particularly talking with the local Londoners, with the result that he had to frequently ask his colleagues to repeat themselves.

One London guy in particular was, by his own admission, difficult to understand:

> I come from the London Essex area, so we do tend to speak quicker than a lot of other English people, and we drop letters making our pronunciation difficult to understand.

Tim also confided that when he first arrived in London, it was as if he was talking to people over a long distance phone line—he only understood something a few seconds after it had been uttered.

When we native speakers don't understand each other, we know it's just a matter of accent; neither party feels stupid or overly embarrassed. But if we can't understand each other, what hope have non-natives got in understanding us?

Basically, accents get in the way of understanding. The key is obviously to enunciate clearly, but you can do much more by raising your own awareness of which elements of your accent typically cause your listeners problems. Go on YouTube and find examples of people imitating (or explaining how to imitate) your accent. For example, the London accent tends (like many other accents in the Anglosphere) to drop the T in *data, automate, twenty* and so on, and the *G* at the end of the word (*running, developing*), and the TH often turns into D or F. In my opinion, no one should be forced to change his/her accent, but just having an awareness of the difficulties it may cause may be useful.

While we native speakers accept that it is normal not to understand each other's unfamiliar accents, when non-natives fail to communicate successfully with native English speakers, they frequently assume it is because of their own poor English skills. Such failures can be demotivating at best, but are often also embarrassing, frustrating, and even humiliating. Sue Osada trains native English speakers to teach English to Japanese students. She offers some useful observations on what we as native speakers need to do to help our listeners understand us better:

> I always have to raise these teachers' awareness to the fact that learners have been mainly exposed to English through standardized

textbook recordings of clear-speaking actors and actresses reading simplified scripts and through Japanese English teacher models. The learners are thus likely to have great difficulty when encountering regional accents, informal register, colloquial structures/expressions, high-speed "youth-speak," and the like. These native-speaker teachers, hence, need to modify their normal spoken variety accordingly. For example, when observing team-teaching lessons in Japan, not only the students, but also the experienced Japanese English teachers often seem thrown by the speed, informality, slang, accents, and so on, of the young native-speaking assistant English teachers!

Here are some tips to help non-natives understand you better when you are talking to them.

- Don't use contracted forms, so say: *This is not, we cannot* (rather than *isn't, can't*).
- Don't be lazy with your pronunciation. Make an effort to enunciate words clearly, don't drop letters.
- Avoid slang such as *bucks* and *quid* for *dollars* and *pounds*.
- Make sure that you have the person's attention. Then if you see any degree of hesitation at all in the person's expression, try to explain again as simply as possible.
- If you find that you are talking in an excited manner, slow down.
- Try to avoid verbal mannerisms, for example, repeatedly saying *you know, like, kind of, I mean*. These phrases tend to be spoken quickly and slurred, so the non-native is not actually able to filter them out as simply being fillers and may think they contain important information.

3.5 I sometimes find it hard to understand English spoken in a foreign language—What can I do?

The Chinese have two different words for "listen," and each word is made up of different symbols, which include a door, an eye, an ear, and a king.

Taken in combination these symbols mean that a listener in China should give the speaker (the king) their undivided attention, through their eyes not just their ears. You should do the same, and you will find that this approach will be the "doorway" to understanding.

Listening to someone speaking English with a nonstandard pronunciation can be hard work. The effort you need to make is also in relation to how familiar you are with the accent of the speaker. If until now you have been used to hearing the English of Spanish speakers, then listening to a Chinese speaker maybe considerably more difficult. The English pronunciation mistakes of the Spanish speakers will be totally different from those of a Chinese person. This means it may take you several hours or several encounters before you tune in to a Chinese accent.

If you can't understand a particular word, get them to write it down. For example, a difficult sound for most non-natives is the *th* in *think* or *north*. So if the word that they write down contains *th*, notice how they pronounce it—does it sound more like a *t* or an *f* or a *d*? When they say another word with *th* in it, and you know that they pronounce *th* as *t*, then if, for example, you hear *tausend* you can guess that what they mean is *thousand*.

If you are finding it really hard to understand, don't look away as this will be interpreted as being a lack of interest in what they are saying, which could be considered offensive. Instead, muster your concentration and hang in there—in the long run you will understand more and more.

Finally, remember that the effort you are making to understand them will be no more than they effort they are probably making to understand you!

3.6 When talking, what kind of vocabulary and expressions should I use and which should I avoid?

The following table highlights what you can do to make yourself more understandable simply by choosing those words and expressions that are more likely to be familiar or understandable for your non-native counterparts.

AREA OF DIFFICULTY	HARD TO UNDERSTAND	MORE LIKELY TO BE UNDERSTOOD
Verb + *up, down, in, out, off,* etc	Beef up; Buy into; Get out of	Make more interesting/longer etc; Believe, agree with; Avoid
Colloquial phrases	Two o'clock works for me. Tops! I so don't want to do this. Cheers, mate; you're a star! It's all gone Peter Tong. A bit iffy.	Two o'clock would suit me. Great! Fantastic! I really don't want to do this. Thank you, you've been really helpful. Unfortunately, everything has gone wrong. Doubtful/Full of uncertainty.
Phrases without a subject	Been having problems with ... Any chance of ... Fancy a drink tonight ... ?	I have been having problems with ... Is there any chance of ...? Would you like a drink ...?

If you are from the United States, you may not even recognize some of the phrases shown as they are very British. Likewise there are many expressions in American English that would be hard for other native speakers of English, and practically impossible for non-natives. So try to avoid US sports expressions (*ballpark, curveball, the gloves are off, homestretch, on the ropes, swim lane, touch base, etc.*) and US business talk (*boil the ocean, drill down, move the needle, open the kimono, put on the backburner, reach out*). The problem with such expressions is that the non-native may not understand that they are indeed expressions, that is, a group of words that in combination have a single meaning. Instead they may try to decipher each word individually and then be left totally confused.

Of course, many expressions and words are so ingrained in our personal mode of speaking (or in the corporate jargon of where we work) that we may not even be aware that they make little sense to someone outside our immediate circle. So when talking to someone, simply look at their facial expression and if it suddenly goes vacant then reword what you've just said. Continue this facial monitoring throughout your conversations, and keep on checking that they've understood.

For more on the types of words to use and avoid (see Sections 2.7, 4.3, and 5.6).

3.7 How can I talk to my foreign clients without "dumbing down" my English?

Staph Bakali, a former COO of the Clinton Health Access Initiative, was born in Morocco and moved to England when he was 11. Over the years, he also learned French and Spanish. This has helped him enormously in communicating with foreign customers, as he is fully aware of the difficulties that they have in terms of understanding native English speakers.

He explained to me how he adapts his English to the situation required:

> When, for example, I am explaining orally what my company does to scientists and subject matter experts I might say: *We are able to screen all open reading frames of any disease-causing agent.*

> But to potential foreign investors, I know that if I say the sentence above quickly it will just sound like a series of noises. Instead, I have to speak in a way my 11-year-old son can understand—that doesn't mean dumbing down what I want to say, but speaking more slowly, giving examples and frequently checking that they have understood me. The result is that clients really appreciate the fact that I am making an effort to help them understand me.

> In my work experience, I have seen so many presentations given by Americans and Brits that left the non-native element in the audience completely frustrated because they only managed to understand a quarter or less of what was said. This has a serious negative effect on future collaborations, as clearly everyone needs to feel that they are being given equal consideration.

In summary:

- The words you use very much depend on who you are talking to, irrespective of whether or not they are a fellow native speaker but particularly so with a non-native.
- Don't use "pidgin English" (see Section 3.2), instead just speak slowly, give plenty of examples, and constantly check that your listener is understanding.

- The more your listeners understand, the better the image you promote of yourself and your business, and the better future relations will be.

3.8 How can I communicate effectively on the phone?

Phone calls are one of the most stressful forms of communication in English for non-native speakers. So first of all consider whether your phone call is really necessary, and whether it wouldn't be simpler, at least for your counterpart, for you to send an email or fax.

If you really need to talk (rather than email), then use Skype or an equivalent. Skype has very useful automatic translation and messaging features. These will considerably enhance your interlocutor's understanding of what you are saying and will also make the phone conversation less stressful.

Assuming that the call is strictly necessary, announce who you are slowly and clearly. If you have a name with a nonobvious pronunciation, like Glynne Hughes or Heather Cowburn, then spell it out—names such as these are uncommon in other languages, unlike Robert, David, Steven, Angela, Susan, which probably sound more familiar to a foreign listener. So you can say "This is Glynne Hughes, H-U-G-H-E-S, calling from Acme, A-C-M-E, in Chicago; may I speak to Andrea Coli please."

It's always a good idea to give both the first name and surname of the person you want to speak to. This will give your listener a greater chance of understanding who it is you want.

When spelling a word, make sure you differentiate clearly between easily confused letters such as B and P, and D and T, and N and M. Although there is an International Alphabet, few people are familiar with it, so use, for example, the names of big cities:, B as in Barcelona, P as in Paris. Always repeat the spelling and always do so slowly.

If you need to leave a message, then speak very slowly and clearly. Repeat each bit of information at least twice, particularly any numbers. When mentioning days of the week, especially Tuesday and Thursday which are very easily confused, always say the day with the date: "Thursday the 16th," so that there's a greater chance of being understood.

At the end of the message get the other person to read the information back to you. Don't say "Would you mind reading that back to me please." Although polite, that particular sentence is unlikely to be understood. Say "Could you repeat that to me please." If there has been a mistake, then clearly indicate the correction—"Sorry, six seven not seven six."

Below are some tips for successful phone calls (for tips on conference calls see Section 5.8).

Ten Tips for Talking on the Phone (Both Outgoing and Incoming Calls)

1. Your interlocutors not only have to switch their brains onto what you're saying but they also have to change language. So give them time to tune into to your voice—just a little small talk (including personal chit chat will help to oil communications between you).

2. Put the person at ease at the start of the call: *Tell me to stop if I'm speaking too quickly or if you don't understand something.* And at the end: *If you need any clarifications, then ring me back or email me.*

3. Speak slowly. This doesn't mean just putting pauses between each word, it also means clearly articulating each individual word in as natural a way as possible. Be careful not to cut out words in your sentences in an attempt to make it simpler.

4. Keep your questions short but clear, particularly when interacting with someone on a helpdesk. So rather than *Just so that I am clear, would you mind explaining the problem again, please?* You could simply say *So the problem is?*

5. When your interlocutor asks you to repeat what you've just said (because he/she doesn't understand), instead of saying the same words louder, use different words in a shorter sentence spoken slowly.

6. Stress the most important points clearly—repeat them several times.

7. Make frequent summaries. If you cannot understand what is being said, then either suggest that the person email you (if he/she has called you), or you could put on the line a colleague that speaks the person's language.

8. Ask lots of questions: *Is that clear? Is there anything you didn't understand? Do you need me to repeat that? Am I speaking too quickly? Have you got any questions?* Could *you to tell me what you've understood so far?*

9. Never try to rush the phone call—give the other person time to digest information.

10. Offer to email a short summary of the main points after the phone call.

3.9 What should I do when I realize (but they don't) that they haven't understood?

Several years ago I carried out a survey for an Italian IT company about how their customers at Salomon Brothers, Goldman Sachs, and Barclays Capital perceived the Italian phone helpline. My interviewees highlighted two key issues.

The first issue is that the helpline operators will tend to home in on just the technical words, without getting the full sense but just what they <u>think</u> is the gist. This means that they assume that the technical word they heard is the source of the customer's problem. For example, let's imagine you have a software problem and you are getting error message 30. Before telephoning the helpline, you investigate error message 30 and discover that this is not the source of your problem. You then ring the helpline hoping to discover the real source. Below is an extract from a typical dialog that highlights what can go wrong:

You: I have a problem with xyz and I'm getting error message 30. The thing is that ...
They: Oh, error message 30, I'll just look that up for you.
You: No, that's not what I want, I've looked it up, it's something else, can we check out something else?
They: OK, error message 30 means that you ...

What happens is that often helpline operators do not have perfect English. When they realize that they have understood a keyword, they latch onto that word. You, in the meantime, get frustrated and blurt out that that is not actually what you are interested in, but you say that so quickly that the helpdesk operator doesn't even hear it and continues with their first line of action. A better approach might be:

> *You*: I have a problem with xyz. Before you give me a solution, I would like to explain what I have already tried to do to solve the problem. Is that OK with you?
> *They*: Yes. Of course.
> *You*: The error message is 30. But I have already discovered that that is NOT the problem.
> *They*: Oh, error message 30, let me just look that up ....
> *You (interrupting before they can continue, but speaking slowly and calmly)*: Sorry, no. Error message 30 is <u>not</u> the problem. I have already checked 30 and it is <u>not</u> the problem. What I need you to do is to find the real problem. Could you just repeat to me what you have understood so far?
> *They*: You get 30, but that's not the problem.

Asking them to repeat what they think they have understood benefits both them and you—they won't waste their own time going down the wrong path, and you increase the chances of being given a solution.

The other key issue is the way you yourself communicate. My interviewees were traders at banks using a software application produced by my Italian client. Traders can have major problems if the software they are using blocks, it means opportunities wasted and possibly vast sums of money lost. In such situations of pressure, we tend to speak very fast. Clearly rapid speech spoken with a great sense of urgency will also throw your interlocutor into a panic. So despite the heat of the moment, speak slowly and clearly, and try to phrase the questions in such a way to make it easy for the operator to reply.

Alternatively go down a route that bypasses the helpline. For example, if your counterpart's company is very responsive to emails, then email is often a better option.

I finished each interview with the traders by remarking that the Italian helpline operators were making a lot of effort to learn English, and asked them: *Do you think you are making the same kind of effort to make yourself understood?* The typical reply was *No, they're definitely making more effort than we are. But we aren't going to learn Italian, so it's up to them; it's unfortunate but true.*

Yes, it <u>is</u> up to them, but that doesn't stop you from trying to make it easier for them. In the end both sides will benefit.

For more on improving your oral communication technique, see Section 5.7.

3.10 When I need to give an instruction or make a criticism, should I adopt a direct or indirect approach?

A polite and indirect way of saying something can be lost on some non-natives. Rajiv Khan from India remembers a time at college in the United States when he was playing his music really loud. The guy in the next room came in and said "that's a nice music system." Rajiv took this as a compliment and was very proud, whereas the guy was actually trying to tell him to turn the music down (this was revealed to Rajiv by a third person who was also present).

This means that a phrase such as: *Can you please do this...* (rather than a more direct: *Please do this...*) could be considered as an option by someone in India if this instruction came from someone at the same level in their hierarchy. However if such an instruction phrased in this polite way came from someone high up, then they would be more likely to carry it out.

Rajiv also informed me that:

> Indians tend not to use polite expressions such as *sorry, please,* and *thank you,* when these are considered unnecessary as in the ordinary course of daily life. However, they *will* apologize if they have done something deliberately that they shouldn't have done.

This means that we cannot expect our counterparts to react in a way that follows our own norms of behavior.

Many non-natives often miss the subtlety of English communication, and in a work environment they may need to be told things directly and upfront. Below is an extract from a guide written for Dutch executives to interpret the underlying meaning of the cryptic phrases of their British colleagues.

WHAT THE BRITISH SAY	WHAT IS UNDERSTOOD BY THE DUTCH	WHAT THE BRITISH ACTUALLY MEAN
Oh, by the way...	This is not very important.	The primary purpose of our discussion is.
I hear what you say.	He/She accepts my point of view.	I disagree and do not want to discuss it any further.
Perhaps you would like to think about ...	Think about the idea, but do what you like.	This is an order. Do it or be prepared to justify yourself.
That is an original point of view.	They like my ideas!	You must be mad.

Clearly, the guide is humorous, but it pays to say what you really mean in a direct (but polite and diplomatic) format. You cannot expect your non-native counterpart to read through the lines and work out your real intended meaning.

But, when you need to give critical feedback to someone, don't go to the other extreme and be too direct. These suggestions may help you balance these two extremes:

- Do not to leap to conclusions. Maybe something was not done or was done badly simply because the person involved didn't even know what had to be done, or maybe the person had something more urgent going on in life.
- Phrase your criticism in a way that it seems that you are also acknowledging that you too may have some responsibility for what has happened.
- Use a constructive tone and always find something positive to say about the other person (preferably both at the beginning and end of your conversation).
- Always leave the dialog open.

For more on resolving difficulties, see Section 2.5.

The impact on your interlocutor of what you say will depend massively on your tone of voice and your facial expression. If it seems to your interlocutor that you have a negative attitude toward him/her, this negativity will override what you are saying even if you are actually saying something positive.

Top Tips

- All conversations are two-way, so it is your responsibility to help your non-native interlocutor understand what you are saying along with trying to understand what he/she is saying. Most native speakers find it difficult to follow a spoken question or statement said by another native speaker that consists of more than about 20 words. So imagine how difficult it might be for your non-native interlocutor to follow you.
- Don't let previous conversation failures or breakdowns with non-native speakers negatively impact all future communication: they or you may have simply been tired or stressed.
- Ensure you have clear ideas in your head. If these ideas are not even clear to you, they will be very disorientating for your listener.
- When speaking on whatever occasion, constantly check that your interlocutor is understanding you, not by asking "OK?" but with concrete comprehension questions. Check that you have understood your interlocutors by repeating back what they've said to you.
- When repeating something: don't just say the same thing louder. Instead, try to understand what part it is of what you've said that your interlocutor does not understand.
- Make sure that when you speak slowly, you're not just putting bigger pauses between words, the words themselves need to be slowed down too.
- Don't waffle on about irrelevant stuff. The listener may not be able to distinguish what is relevant from what is not.
- Remember that some words don't sound anything like the way they are written (e.g., *mortgage*). So there's a fair chance

that even if your interlocutor knows the word, he/she might not be able to recognize it in its spoken form.

- Phone calls can be very tiring for a non-native, so before making a phone call decide whether you really need to use the phone. For your non-native counterparts, emails are much easier to understand (they can read them more than once to check understanding) and a record can be kept.

- When phoning: (1) talk slowly and clearly, especially to the receptionist or switchboard operator; (2) spell out names, numbers, and *Tuesday* and *Thursday* (these can sound identical to a non-native)—repeat them several times; (3) always summarize what you've said; (4) be patient; and (5) send an email confirming what you've said.

CHAPTER 4

Reading and Writing

Seven things you didn't know you didn't know

- Researchers at Nielsen Norman Group, which investigates user experiences (including reading habits), have yet to find a single person in the thousands that they have surveyed who has complained that a sentence is too easy to read and that they would have preferred a harder version.
- The top 20 most translated books (i.e., translated into the most different languages) include: *The Bible* (1), *Pinocchio* (2), *The Little Prince* (6), Hans Andersen's Fairy Tales (8), *The Adventures of Asterix* (10), *the Qu'ran* (11), and the *Harry Potter* series (19).
- Early typewriters had the keys in alphabetical order. The most commonly used keys were relocated so that the metal bars attached to the keys wouldn't get trapped together. Hence the QWERTY keyboard.
- According to a national survey of executives, 79 percent listed the ability to write as the most neglected skill in business, and 89 percent believed that clear writing demonstrates clear thinking.
- English spelling can be truly absurd as highlighted by these few lines from a famous poem called "Cork and Work and Card and Ward": *I take it you already know/Of tough and bough and cough and dough?/Others may stumble, but not you/On hiccough, thorough, laugh and through./I write in case you wish perhaps/To learn of less familiar traps:/Beware of heard, a dreadful word/That looks like beard, and sounds like bird./And dead: it's said like bed, not bead; For goodness sake, don't call it 'deed'!*

- Given their short attention spans (one study of university students found that they had an attention span of only 30 seconds!) readers today adopt a power browsing strategy, that is, skimming and scanning through text, looking for key words.
- Japanese has shortened many compound nouns in English: *rimokon* (remote control), *pasokon* (personal computer), *eakon* (air conditioner), *masukomi* (mass communication).

4.1 How well do non-natives write in English?

Translations from a foreign language into English often "look" English but don't "sound" so. Here is an example of an email from a Chinese LED lighting supplier:

Dear who may concerned,
This is Sarah from XYZ Lighting in China, glad to offer the most competitive LED service for you.
XYZ Lighting is aiming at offering series of LED lights with superior quality and competitive prices for our esteemed customers, there's 4 things that seperate us from other suppliers:

1: No MOQ request (any sample orders are warmly welcome)
2: Fastest turnaround time from our factory to our customer
3: Most complete customer care
4: Most competitive price (no hidden costs).

Have a great day!
Sarah

Your conclusion might be that because their English contains many mistakes, this may reflect their general lack of professionalism. This is generally not the case, and the writer is simply formulating a text using the "model" (see Section 1.5) of their own language. By the way, it is common practice for the Chinese to give themselves an English name (e.g., Sarah) as this facilitates relations since the Western counterparts don't have to learn the Chinese pronunciation of the name.

Other times, a particular phrase may stick out as being inappropriate. For example, an Indian textbook on communications skill offers the following advice: *Avoid sending confidential email messages otherwise roving eyes have eye on them.* This kind of mix of formal and informal styles is typical of anyone writing in a language that is not their own.

There are also cases, of course, where non-natives write better English than we do!

4.2 How does English writing differ from other languages?

The way English tends to be written today is reader-focused rather than writer-focused. This means that all the effort is made by the writer to help the reader understand. This is not so in other languages. For example, the connection between thoughts in some languages may only become clear when the whole sentence or paragraph has been read.

In some languages, writers like to perplex their readers with long sentences full of subordinate clauses (i.e., phrases between commas that split up the flow of the main thought) and a series of conjunctions (*notwithstanding, however, in addition, furthermore, nevertheless*). This is often a remnant of their education system in which they may have been taught to demonstrate their command of language by using such a style.

In the past, the way English was written was far more complex. However, unlike in many other countries, businesses and governments in the Anglosphere have realized that by writing simply and clearly they can save money (clear instructions, thus less work for helpdesks) and motivate people to buy products and services (through simple and concise adverts).

Of course, it is dangerous to generalize, and many English writers write in an obscure way, and likewise non-English speakers write in a clear way. There is actually nothing intrinsically more complex in one language with respect to another—the level of complexity of the writing is the choice of the writer, rather than a default of the language.

Even within the Anglosphere, writing styles can differ. The typical style of a US self-help blog with paragraphs of just 1 to 3 sentences and the use of highly colloquial interjections and humorous quips, might irritate many native speakers across the Atlantic, and would be totally lost on non-natives. The type of style I am talking about is:

> Crossing the line. Everyone's talking about it, but no one I know can tell you exactly where the damn line is.
>
> So, a quick definition so we know where we're heading: doing something—physically or verbally—that just ain't appropriate.
>
> (OK OK, I know, that doesn't really clarify anything... yet. But hey, gimme a break. We're just getting the show on the road. Jeez.)

For many natives, the effort involved in reading this style of writing far outweighs any hidden useful information that could be gleaned from it. For a non-native, this type of super informal approach to a serious topic would be impossible to digest. Of course, blogs are meant to be read by like-minded people, and are certainly not aimed at non-natives. But the point I am making is that a colloquial style is much harder for a non-native to understand than a more traditional approach to writing.

4.3 Is it a good idea to use plain English rather than "sophisticated" English?

No, not necessarily.

The Oxford Guide to Plain English, written by one of the Plain English Campaign's founders Martin Cutts, has a list of words that he recommends should not be used in order to avoid being perceived as "pompous, officious, and long-winded."

At the top of the next page are some examples from Cutts' guide, which may work for a native English audience, but not for non-natives.

Instead of	Consider using
accustomed to	used to
additional	more, extra
alleviate	ease
ascertain	find out
attribute	earmark

Martin Cutts and colleagues have helped massively to reduce the amount of bureaucratic balderdash written in the UK and to make forms used by the government, the health service and the legal profession much easier to fill in and process. Similar work has been done in other English-speaking countries. However, what works for a native speaker does not necessarily transfer to a non-native.

In reality, the words in the left-hand column may be more "difficult" or "sophisticated" for your average Brit or American, yet they are far more likely to be understood by a non-native.

Firstly, they often look like a word with a similar meaning in the non-native's language for example, *aliviar* (alleviate) *accertare* (ascertain)*, attribuer* (attribute), in Spanish, Italian and French, respectively. They will thus be easier to understand when a non-native reads them. This is even true for people whose language is totally different from English/Latin. The words that we consider to be more "difficult" are in fact those words that non-natives are likely to have come across in their own reading of English for example, technical manuals, course books, and scientific reports.

Secondly, the left-hand words are also easier to understand when they are spoken. Because they have more syllables, they take longer to say. They thus give the listener more time to absorb them.

Thirdly, the right-hand words may be confusing. For example, to a non-native *I am used to getting up early* (i.e., I am accustomed) sounds and looks very similar to *I used to get up early* (but now I get up at a normal time). Such subtleties are often lost on non-natives. Saying *I am accustomed to getting up early* may sound rather pompous, but it will give a clearer meaning to the non-native. Another example is *find out*—a non-native who has never heard this verb before would naturally think that *find* and *out* are two distinct concepts with separate meanings, rather than just a single verb. Other similar verbs (see Section 2.7) to avoid would be: *get out of* (avoid), *get off on* (enjoy), *give up* (stop), *take on* (engage), *dream up* (invent), that is, any verb + short word (*on, off, up, down, in, out, for*, etc.). However, some are used so commonly that a non-native *will* recognize and use them for example, *I look forward to seeing you* (frequently used as a salutation in emails), *start up* (set up/initiate a new business).

Finally, the right-hand words, which tend to have Anglo-Saxon origins, are often more colorful but consequently more confusing to a non-native. What would they make of *earmark*? Logically it could be interpreted as meaning a mark on one's ear, though a native speaker would probably know that it comes from the pre-Kindle era when people marked an important passage in a book by folding over the top corner of the page. Such words are thus likely to confuse a non-native, who might try to make out the meaning of the word from its constituent parts.

In summary, although other experts such as James Aitchison in his book *The Cassell Guide to Written English*, state that *monosyllabic words often have qualities of immediacy and simplicity; likely to be more familiar and intelligible than abstract and polysyllabic nouns*, it is actually the polysyllabic words that non-natives will find easier to manage and may tend to use themselves.

The following table shows a list of words of Anglo Saxon origins and their Latin equivalents (though not necessarily with exactly the same meaning). Whereas you might prefer to use the Anglo Saxon words with fellow native speakers, your foreign interlocutors might find the Latin ones easy to recognize and understand (see Section 2.7).

Anglo Saxon	Latin	Anglo Saxon	Latin
bolster	support	put down	humiliate
childish	infantile	reckless	irresponsible
clue	indication	self-same	identical
forbid	prohibit	span	distance
irk	irritate	wish	desire
loathe	detest	worthy	valuable

This does not mean that you should always use a Latin equivalent. For example, *aim* may be just as likely to be understood as *objective*, likewise with: *answer* (response), *ask* (enquire), *friendly* (amicable), *job* (profession), *meet* (encounter), *skillful* (adept), *start* (commence), *watch* (observe). You will agree that these words are very often used, whereas those in the table (*bolster, irk, loathe*) are much less common.

To understand what derives from Latin (or French and Greek) and what does not, look at the number of syllables—for instance the word *syllables* has three *syl-la-bles*, that is, three separate sounds. Generally speaking, the more syllables it has, the more likely it will be comprehensible (in the sense of "heard" easily) to a non-native.

For more ideas on the kind of words to use and to avoid, see Sections 2.7, 4.3, and 5.6.

4.4 Generally speaking, should I opt to use one word rather than three, four, or five?

Yes. Your aim is to help your reader understand with the least effort possible in the shortest amount of time.

For example: *We compared x and y* is shorter and clearer than *We made a comparison of x and y*.

This also means you should avoid long-winded expressions, where a simple one would do.

In his wonderful book *Plain English for Lawyers*, professor of law, Richard Wydick, gives a series of very useful examples to show why and how long sentences should be pruned. Here is an example of typical legal-like verbosity:

> The ruling by the trial judge was prejudicial error for the reason that it cut off cross-examination with respect to issues that were vital. (24 words)

Wydick suggests rewriting it as:

> The trial judge's ruling was prejudicial error because it cut off cross-examination on vital issues. (15 words).

The revamped version is over a third shorter, but nothing is lost in terms of content—all the key words are still there. If a 90-page document could be reduced in this way, it would end up being 60 pages, with massive savings in terms of the reader's effort and time (not to mention printing costs).

However, a few points are worth making:

- *Trial judge's ruling*—this contains three nouns in sequence. Any more than three nouns can lead to confusion for the reader who may not be sure how the individual words relate to each other;
- *Cut off*—its meaning may not be immediately clear to a non-native, so *terminated* or *prevented* might be more helpful;
- *Prejudicial error*—if the audience does not have a legal back-ground, then clearly this would need rephrasing or explain-ing/defining (e.g., a mistake that is made in handling a trial, resulting in harm to the complaining party).

In the same chapter, Wydick has a section entitled *Avoid Compound Constructions*, for example, *then* is clearly preferable to *at that point in time.* He writes: *Every time you see one of these pests on your page, swat it. Use a simple form instead.* He then lists some common examples that can also be found in all books on "good" writing, which include the following:

Compound	Simple
for the reason that	because
in the event that	if
in accordance with	by, under
in favor of	for
in order to	to
with reference to	about, concerning

For a native English speaking audience, Wydick is spot on and severe swatting is required. However, in some cases for a non-native the situation is different. The words *because* and *if* are absolutely fine—basically they have only one meaning, so there can be no difficulty of interpretation for the reader. However *by, for, to* and *about* are used in hundreds of different cases with many different meanings (*for the moment, for five years, for you, study for an exam*, etc.).

So in cases where you think a word might have many different meanings and could possibly cause confusion, then rather than reaching for your swatter go for the more verbose/pompous alternative—always put clarity first.

4.5 What are readability indexes and how useful are they?
Books such as Professor Wydick's (see Section 4.4) are aimed at making our writing more readable, and they are extremely successful in doing so. There are also software programs that try to do the same, but less successfully.

A readability index is designed to judge the level of difficulty of a document written in English. Readability indexes follow the same principles as the Plain English Campaign (see Section 4.3), so Anglo Saxon words score better than Latinate (polysyllabic) ones, active sentences (*I did x*) are preferred to passive ones (*x was done*), and short sentences fare better than long ones. Microsoft Word's grammar check follows the same principles.

Again, readability indexes are designed to help us—native speakers—communicate better with our fellow native speakers. They don't always work with non-natives.

My advice would be:

- Yes, opt for short sentences provided they are clear and unambiguous (see Section 4.6).
- Yes, use the active form where possible—but don't be obsessed by this; there are plenty of occasions when the passive is more appropriate (i.e., when we don't know or don't care who did the action).
- Ignore any prompts to choose a monosyllabic word over a polysyllabic one (see Sections 2.7 and 4.3).

4.6 How does ambiguity arise and what can I do about it?

Many cases of ambiguity arise because the words are not in the best order, or because a key word can have more than one meaning. This is highlighted by these newspaper headlines:

A quarter of a million Chinese live on water

Astronaut takes blame for gas in spacecraft

Children hit as teachers strike

Dealers will hear car talk at noon

Enraged cow injures farmer with axe

Juvenile court to try shooting defendant

Kids make nutritious snacks

Killer sentenced to die for second time in 10 years

Police found drunk in shop window

Red tape holds up new bridge

In addition to infelicitous word order, be careful of:

- Latin words and abbreviations—for example, many people (including native speakers) are unsure of the difference between *e.g.* and *i.e.*
- *The former* and *the latter* to refer back to something that you wrote before. For example, if I write *the Greeks, Turks, Italians and Japanese all have a tendency to write convoluted sentences blah blah blah blah blah blah blah blah. However, the former also ...* I am forcing you to read backwards so that you can remember who *the former* refers to, and even then you may not be sure if it refers just to the Greeks (or to the Greeks and Turks, or maybe even the Greeks, Turks and Italians). The best solution is to repeat the key word (*However, the Turks also ....*)
- *It, them, this, these,* etc., when it is not entirely clear what these words refer to. The problem is the same as with *the former* and *the latter* (see previous point), and is a recurrent problem in emails
- Uncommon words—for example, to prove this point I deliberately used the word *infelicitous* in introducing this list of bullets. The term *infelicitous* only gets 350,000 results on Google, whereas easier alternatives such as *unfortunate* and *inappropriate* get 80 million and 678 million, respectively. If you stick to common words, you massively increase the chances of your reader understanding them

When you have finished writing an important document or email, ensure that someone else reads it. A second pair of eyes will more likely spot potential ambiguity.

4.7 What the hell are false friends? And should I be worried about them?

Imagine you received an email that said:

I am not clear about the *argument* of your email. *Eventually* could you give me more specific details of the times of the flights so that I can put them in my *agenda*?

You might not be clear about what exactly the sender meant by their use of the words in italics. This is because these words are "false friends"—they are words that are spelt similarly in English and another language, but have different meanings. In most European languages *argument* means "topic," *eventually* means "if necessary," and *agenda* means a "diary."

Here are some other words that often cause confusion. In brackets is the way that a word with a very similar spelling is used in many other European languages:

> *actually* (currently), *assist* (take part, attend), *canteen* (cellar), *concourse* (competitive examination), *control* (check), *convenient* (cheap) *education* (good manners, what you learn at home), *fabric* (factory), *journal* (daily newspaper), *library* (book shop), *magazine* (warehouse), *occasion* (opportunity), *preservative* (contraceptive), *realize* (create, develop), *sensible* (sensitive), *sympathetic* (friendly)

In the confusing cases above, the difference in meaning arises because the languages involved have a Latin element. One language may have conserved the original Latin meaning, whereas the same word in another language may have taken a different course and ended up meaning something different.

False friends also arise when one language adopts the word of another country and then uses it in a different way—for example, *latte* in Italian simply means *milk*, not a type of coffee (the confusion arose because the Italian *caffe latte* means a coffee with milk). Japanese has a totally different origin from English but has adopted many English words including *hafu* (half) = mixed race; *konpurekkusu* (complex) = inferior complex; *rinsu* (rinse) = hair conditioner; *sumato* (smart) = slim; and *torena* (trainer) = sweat shirt.

So what can you do?

- Be aware of the existence of false friends. When you meet a word in a non-native's written text, and this word appears to be out of context, check on the Web whether it might be a false friend.

- Develop an interest in other languages—false friends are a fascinating area of language learning.
- If you are going to be working with someone who speaks a specific language, for example, Russian, then Google: "Russian English false friends." You will then see lists of such words, which you could try to avoid in your dealings with your Russian collaborators.

Of course, I recognize that my recommendations entail a certain amount of effort on your part, for which you simply may not have the time.

4.8 How bothered do I need to be about punctuation?

Dzongkha, the official language of the Kingdom of Bhutan, has no punctuation. Not only that, all the words are joined together. As a result, it is very difficult to read and segregate letters into words. Here is an example taken from Wikipedia; it is the first two sentences of Article 1 of the declaration of human rights.

ༀ། །འགྲོ་བ་མི་རིགས་ག་ར་དབང་ཆ་འདྲ་མཉམ་འབད་སྒྱེ་ལས་ག་ར་གིས་གཅིག་གིས་གཅིག་ལུ་སྤུན་ཆ་དེ་དང་ཚོད་བརྩན་དགོས།

And here is an example of a short handwritten text:

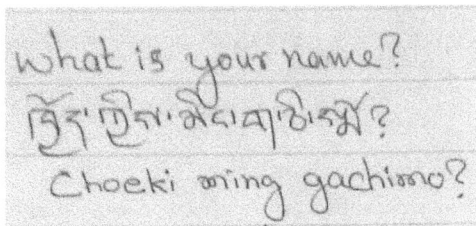

The first documents to be written in Latin (and English and many other languages) also had no punctuation, no spacing between words. But why?

When writing began, knowledge was intended to be in the hands of the few, essentially the clergy.

In Christianity, the New Testament preaches equality. However in order for the elite to maintain power and justify their privileged position, they had to prevent the true Christian message from being spread, and also prevent others from reading the documents that the elite wrote for each other. Readingatextwithnopunctuationandspacesishardwork, so eventually spaces and rudimentary punctuation were introduced. The advent of printing aided this process. But books cost a lot. So only the privileged few could read them. Then came newspapers. The *New York Times* today is written so that a 17-year-old can understand it easily. Not so a hundred years ago. Information was still the domain of the few. In fact, the cost of newspapers was relatively prohibitive so that the masses could not afford to buy them. The elite still wanted an exclusive on information.

This carried on well into the 20th century. When the Germans lost the second world war, some of their retreating armies ended up in Italy. Soldiers, captains and generals hid in Italian houses. A Wehrmacht commander abandoned his books in a house in Tuscany, among which was the *Deutsche Bibel* translated by Martin Luther, the family Bible of every German. In fact it was the first bible that had ever been seen in that house. Incredibly, in 1945, Italians were not allowed to read the bible without the bishop's written permission. At that time, between 3 and 32 percent of the Italian population were illiterate (depending on the region), so the majority of people did in fact have the skills to read the Bible but were simply not allowed to.

So in a certain sense, writing, and by extension, punctuation, is power.

If you don't use punctuation (correctly), you are keeping information to yourself.

If you use it well, you will reach out to a wide audience.

But this little bit of history also highlights a significant difference between Protestants and Catholics. Luther translated his Bible into German 500 years ago. This meant that Germans could read the Bible in their own tongue—the idea was to spread the message with little concern into whose hands the message fell. Luther sparked off the Reformation by saying that there should be no intermediary priests between God and the faithful—instead people should have full direct access to knowledge. In England too, the Bible was translated into English. But in Catholic countries the Bibles that were made available were in Latin—so very few could understand them (Latin was practically a dead language). In 1945 versions of the Bible did exist in Italian, but they weren't publicly available and could only be accessed in the presence of some authority.

To some extent this explains the slightly different attitudes to what the purpose of writing is in northern and southern Europe (and consequently also in North America and South America). Italy has no real equivalent of the Plain English Campaign (see Section 4.3), instead it has an academy to "protect" the language. At the risk of making a massive generalization, it could be said that in Protestant countries people expect to be informed and to have access to information that is written for them in a language they can understand. This is not necessarily the case in Catholic countries, where many documents are written in such a way that information (and thus knowledge) is shrouded in complex phrases rather than being imparted clearly.

In reality, any writers from any country can make life difficult for their readers. Lawyers of all nationalities tend to write in a way that can only be interpreted by them—in this case knowledge breeds money.

So, enough of history. What do you make of this?

> In a Latin examination James where John had had had had had had had had had had the examiner's approval.

That's eleven *hads* in a row! If you can't work out how to punctuate to reveal its hidden meaning, then look at the key at the end of this chapter. Clue: Imagine that James and John have to translate the Latin *habuerat* (= had had) into English: James gets it right (*had had*) and John gets it wrong (*had*).

Punctuation enables your readers to make sense of what you are saying. Some other classic cases that highlight the differences that punctuation marks can make are as follows:

1. Charles I walked and talked ten days after he was beheaded.
2. Police help dog bite victim.
3. A clever dog knows its master.

See the key at the end of this chapter. For more on punctuation, see Section 2.10.

4.9 How should I use punctuation in technical documentation and report writing?

Punctuation shows the grammatical relationships between words, phrases, and sentences. It is also used to regulate pace, to highlight particular words, and to show thought dependence. As a test for clarity, try removing the punctuation from a sentence. If it doesn't make sense anyway, it probably needs rephrasing, especially if it has a lot of commas.

In technical writing it is best to use short, concise sentences so that the meaning becomes clearer. Basically you only need commas and full stops. If there are more than two items in a list, use a comma before *and*. This helps to underline the relationships before the various elements in the list. So write *X, Y, and Z*. Don't write: ~~X, Y and Z~~.

Use a semicolon to divide up the elements in a list into groups. If I write *We did A, B and C, and D and E* it is not clear whether there are two steps (A+B+C and D+E) or three steps (A then B+C then D+E). So instead write: *We did A; B and C; and D and E.*

In any case, lists can often be visualized better in bullets rather than as text. So rather than writing *We installed X and Y; Q, R and S; B and C;* and *D*, it would be clearer if you wrote:

> The following were installed:
>
> - X and Y
> - Q, R and S
> - B and C

Use hyphens to reveal the meaning of potential ambiguous phrases. For example, *a little-used car* is a car that has not been used very much. *A little used-car* is a small second-hand car.

Use a comma when providing additional information about something.

> My boss who works in Paris is German. = I have more than one boss and I am just referring to the one who works in Paris, rather than the ones who work in Berlin and Rome.

> My boss, who works in Paris, is German. = I only have one boss. The fact that she works in Paris is only incidental information.

Use commas to avoid possibility ambiguity. There is a very fine distinction between the following two sentences, but there are cases where such a distinction may be crucial.

> More and more Australians are traveling solo. = an increasing number of Australians
> More and more, Australians are traveling solo. = an increasing trend

Finally, brackets tend to invite the reader to skip the phrase inside the brackets. So remove the info from the brackets if you want to ensure that it is registered.

4.10 I am writing a technical manual. What do I need to be aware of?
There's a joke in the technical writing world that goes like this:

> *How to defuse a bomb*

> Step 1: Cut the red wire.

> Step 2: Make sure that you've cut the green wire before proceeding with Step 1.

This joke is often used in technical writing courses to encourage budding manual writers to list information in the order a user needs to know it, which is also known as "just in-time information." The underlying idea is: would you trust your own writing if it were used for a bomb disposal procedure? The joke clearly illustrates that instructions should follow a chronological order. And this is obviously true for whoever you are writing for—native or non-native.

Here are some other guidelines, which are simply good rules of writing and applicable to all readers:

14 Guidelines for Writing Technical Documents

1. Think about what is it that readers need to know and give them only that.

2. Don't make assumptions—think about the prior information readers will need in order to be able to understand and follow your instructions.

3. Say what your product or service actually does, not just what it is designed to do.

4. If you are instructing readers on how to assemble a product, tell readers what tools they might need and provide tips as you go along. Both the tools and tips can be put in a shaded box or in a column alongside the main text.

5. Have only one instruction in each sentence. Limit yourself to one idea per sentence and avoid long sentences. Avoid long blocks of text and long paragraphs.

6. When describing a procedure, tell the reader about the expected results of each step; don't leave them in suspense.

7. When giving warnings: (1) Don't be afraid to repeat negation words such as *not* and *never,* and (2) explain the consequences of ignoring a warning.

8. Avoid slang, unnecessary jargon, and idiomatic expressions.

9. Make it clear to the reader whether he/she has to do something, or whether the software/device does something automatically.

10. Don't force your readers to work things out—don't tax their brains. Structure your documents so that readers can intuitively locate everything. If your organization produces a lot of documents on similar subjects, ensure the documents look the same, have the same structure, and use the same terminology. This means that readers will be able to understand the content much more easily.

11. Remember that manuals are often used in situations of stress (i.e., when something has gone wrong). Try to reduce this stress by helping your readers assimilate the information in a relaxed way.

12. Make your guides and manuals satisfying to use and consult.
13. Remember that diagrams and photos often speak louder than words.
14. Put clarity and precision before conciseness.

By following these 14 guidelines, you will also make your document much easier to translate into other languages. If you are going to be writing a lot of manuals, then you might be interested in my book *User Guides, Manuals, and Technical Writing* (Springer).

Key Tips

- According to the Oxford Dictionaries website there are between a quarter and three quarters of a million words in the English language—depending on how you classify the term "word" and whether you include technical words. So there are lots of synonyms available for you to choose from: prefer words that you think may derive from Latin or French for example, *difficult* (multisyllable) rather than *hard* (monosyllable)—these tend to be easier to understand for non-natives, whatever their native language.
- Readability indexes are not necessarily useful when you have a non-native English speaking audience, nor are guidelines regarding how to write plain English.
- Cut your non-native counterparts some slack when reading their documents. The same document that might take you an hour to write could take them a couple of days. Don't be surprised if they inadvertently use a mix of styles, for example, very informal expressions followed suddenly by what may seem to be some erudite or rather pompous-sounding vocabulary.
- Always provide a focused message. Think about your readers, and make it simpler for them to understand quickly at one reading. Don't use complex language in order to sound smart.
- Less than 5 percent of readers can understand a 27-word sentence at the first reading. Divide up long sentences into

shorter sentences, and opt for words that only have one meaning. This is particularly important when writing user guides and manuals.

- Remove redundant words and phrases, and be concise, but not too concise—your meaning must always be clear. Research has shown that more readers stop reading in the first 50 words than they do in the following 250 words.
- When writing user manuals or medical leaflets, imagine that you are talking to the reader: explain all technical language, use active sentences, explain every step of a procedure, and provide the expected outcome.
- Avoid ambiguity.
- Use punctuation to make your meaning clear.
- Try learning a bit of the language of your counterparts, you will soon see the similarities between English and their language, and this will help you in your choice of the right word.

Key to 4.8:
In a Latin examination, James, where John had had "had," had had "had had." "Had had" had had the examiner's approval.

Charles I walked and talked. Ten days after he was beheaded. Police help *dog-bite* victim. A clever dog knows *it's* master.

CHAPTER 5

Meetings and Negotiations

Eight things you didn't know you didn't know

- Over a thousand years ago in England (and Scandinavia), the village elders used to meet on a hill or earth mound. This mound was known as a *moot hill*, and in later years *moot halls* were built where knights and sheriffs would make their decisions regarding the local area. So a *moot point* was then, as it is today, an issue open for discussion in a meeting (*moot* and *meet* have a similar etymology).
- In mid-18th century France, people attending a public ceremony used to be given a little ticket or *etiquette*, with instructions for how to behave during the ceremony. Business cards were introduced in Britain in the eighteenth century. In China and Japan, business cards are usually exchanged with both hands, thereby showing your esteem and respect for the other person through the extra effort it takes to use both hands rather than one.
- At meetings in Japan, there are ranks for seats such as *kamiza* the best seat or *shimoza* the most humble seat. There is also a seating order in cars, in an elevator, and in an airplane.
- According to the author of *Murphy's Law*, Arthur Bloch: *If a problem causes many meetings, the meetings eventually become more important than the problem.* And Herbert Beerbohm Tree, British actor-manager quipped that: *A committee should consist of three men, two of whom are absent.*
- C. Northolt Parkinson's "coefficient of inefficiency" calculated that a meeting of just five people was "most likely to act with competence, secrecy, and speed." Few such bodies exist because five swiftly expands to nine: and two of the nine tend

to be "merely ornamental," people whom no one has the heart to exclude.

- The Japanese spend far more on corporate entertainment than do US companies. This may reflect why there's far less litigation over business agreements. In fact, in the United States there are 281 lawyers per 10,000 citizens, in Japan only 7, France 9, and GB 94.

- When holding meetings in Hong Kong and Japan, don't be surprised if some team members take a nap—their colleagues will nudge them when something relevant to them is being discussed.

- In order to avoid speaking English, some non-natives schedule a global meeting that falls during the middle of the night for the native speakers. By doing so, the native speakers are forced to experience some of the anxiety and loss of power typically suffered by the non-native speakers.

5.1 Does every culture view the purpose of a business meeting in the same way?

Most of the western world is very task orientated. So the purpose of a meeting is usually clearly understood, as is the hierarchy of the people involved in the decision making. In contrast the Japanese, for example, do not necessarily enter discussions or meetings expecting to come up with an outcome or a solution, and they don't expect an individual to necessarily come up with the answer. The answer will often arise by the individuals participating in the discussions and in allowing time to come up with the right solution.

Just because someone is attending your meeting, he/she may not have necessarily been delegated to deliver the solution. For example, Japan has a group-oriented culture, so harmony and cooperation inside the group is very important. There is a common phrase *Kuuki wo yomu* which literally means "reading the air" and which is key to understanding Japanese culture. While Americans tend to be very direct and not afraid to speak their mind when communicating, Japanese are expected to understand the "atmosphere," the "mood," or the "situation" in the group.

Whereas we might feel awkward around silence, in Japanese business meetings silence (see Section 5.10) maintains harmony within the group and may serve to release the tension in the room.

As usual, don't assume that all Asians, or even all Japanese, will adopt the same approach as outlined earlier. The way business is conducted on a multinational level is becoming more and more uniform.

5.2 How does management style influence the way people of a certain culture conduct meetings and negotiations?

Imagine you are going to a meeting at another company in your own country, attended by people exclusively from your own country. Before the meeting you are likely to have discussions with your colleagues of this type:

> I have heard the CFO is a bit ... We may need to think of a strategy to deal with this.

> I know the sales manager, and she's very flexible, in fact a good approach would be to ...

> Apparently, they recently lost a client because ..., so maybe we could leverage this in our favor ...

In fact, you might well have the same conversations with your colleagues before a meeting in your own company with your own group. And you'd be wise to do a bit of personality assessment before going into a family meeting to discuss your ageing parents, moving house, where to go on holiday, and so on.

To a great extent, the management style operative in a country is just a variation of the management style operated within a company or family ... and of course not all companies and not all families are the same. For example, how you manage your children is obviously not identical to the way another family in your country manages their children, and may in fact be very different due to your different values (political, religious, etc.) and personalities (e.g., strict, tolerant, permissive).

In any case, it may help to do a bit of background work before doing business with a new company overseas. A guidebook to doing business in the Middle East, for example, might tell you:

> When conducting business in Saudi Arabia, you are likely to notice a greater power distance. In the US and the UK, subordinates would expect to be consulted and to share decisions with their managers. Saudi managers are expected to take full responsibility. On the other hand, we might feel that conflicts within a company can be productive rather than something to avoid.
>
> In Saudi Arabia, people tend to be quite idealistic about their leaders, with a greater sense of loyalty. There is less delegation, and stress may be put on position rather than ability.
>
> In much of the Middle East social obligations often take precedence, and this impacts the way business is done. Things tend to be conducted at a more leisurely and friendly pace, with everything done on a personal level. So Saudis may give preference to people they know and have established a good relationship with. In the Anglosphere, we are often just interested in getting the job done in the quickest time possible, without ever really getting to know our counterparts—so we are more task-oriented, rather than person-oriented.

The information in the preceding passage may or may not be true. For example, the Saudi managers you meet may have been educated at the London School of Economics or the Harvard Business School, or they may have spent years working in New York. So in reality their approach may be no different from yours. Or who knows, maybe you have spent decades in a South American or a Mediterranean country and your approach to business may have been affected by that experience, so that the people-oriented Saudis may fit perfectly with your own style of conducting business.

That is not to say that all information provided by cultural guides should be dismissed. The importance of personal relationships in the Middle East (and in many other parts of the world) is undeniable. Thus speaking in clear English reasonably slowly is going to make you a lot more friends, than rapid speech full of slang (see Section 5.6), which is likely to alienate your listeners. Also, knowing that people come first in much of the Middle East is likely to affect your socializing style—see Chapter 8.

But at the end of the day, and very generally speaking, it all boils down to personality. If you can identify the type of personalities you are going to be dealing with, and communicate accordingly, then how you come across to each other as individuals (or as a company as whole) will often override any cultural differences there may be between you.

5.3 How does it feel to be a non-native speaker in a meeting or negotiating? What do I need to be aware of?

Luciano Modica, a professor of mathematics and former Italian senator, has considerable experience in meeting native English speakers both in the academic and political worlds. He told me this:

> International relations are particularly difficult to accomplish in a language that is not one's mother tongue: negotiating, joking, discussing. Often our tone of voice sounds wrong to the native English speaking listener. We non-natives are often weaker in negotiations, or less witty, or more aggressive than we actually wish to be. Yet spontaneity and direct dialogue are indispensable to create the personal trust that is the basis of every human relationship. In a globalized society we need to think carefully about identifying the best strategies to ensure, from a language point of view, the maximum equality of opportunity between the various stakeholders.

On the other side of the table are the native speakers. Michelle Hopkins is a Canadian travel journalist. She shared some tips with me on how to improve communication with non-native English speakers:

> I have learned that effective communication depends on three things: (1) not making any equation on a conscious or subconscious level between someone's ability to speak English and their level of intelligence; (2) taking responsibility for any lack of understanding by my interlocutor by speaking slowly and using words

that I feel sure they are more likely to understand—the fact that I also speak French means that if I am speaking to someone whose language is similar to French, for example, Spanish or Italian, I will use English words that I know are similar to words in their own language; and (3) making frequent summaries of both what I have said and of what I believe the other person has said to me.

English entrepreneur Martin Gandy worked in the pulp paper business for several decades in Germany, Finland, and Italy. He told me:

I don't speak other languages. Fortunately, most people I deal with speak English very well. But they don't like colloquialism and they don't like complicated language. So I speak to people slowly and use simple language. I ensure that I have the person's attention, and if I see any degree of hesitation at all in their expression, then I explain again.

Michelle and Martin mention several simple strategies to improve communication:

- Don't equate English level with intelligence level
- Speak slowly choosing the best words (see Section 4.3)
- Avoid colloquial expressions
- Carefully observe and react to your counterpart's body language
- When repeating an explanation, ensure you simplify it rather than complicating it
- Make frequent summaries

5.4 Does the concept of a "negotiation" vary from country to country?
Most words have a near correspondence between one language and another. The actual meanings of even abstract words such as *love, freedom, performance*, and *professionalism* do not vary massively. "Negotiation" is a big exception—it has extremely different connotations from language to language, and culture to culture. Our word, which is practically the same word in French, Spanish, Portuguese, and Italian, literally means "not leisure," i.e., work/business. The German, Dutch, and Scandinavian

words are a little more direct: they talk about "handling" (*handeln*)—you can imagine the two parties in a negotiation physically handling the merchandize as well as metaphorically handling the situation and each other. The Arabic word, مُفاوَضة (mufawada) on the other hand is derived from a verb تفاوضَ (tafawad) which means discussing a conflict to reach a satisfying point.

Just as our word *negotiation* is made up of two parts, so too are the words for *negotiation* of various oriental languages. In languages with ideograms, an individual word can either express the meaning explicitly by itself, or describe a concept using combination of several other words.

LANGUAGE	TWO PART WORD	MEANING
English, French, Spanish, Portuguese, Italian, Romanian	Latin: neg + otium	no + idleness
Chinese	谈判 (tán pàn)	seek an agreed solution for an issue that is the concern of more than one representative, through discussion and the exchange of judgments
Japanese	kosho	mix + concern/relationship
Vietnamese	àm phán	discuss/talk + make decision
Hindi	sulajh + jana	resolve + make happen

Knowing that negotiation means different things to different people, and may not necessarily imply there has to be some fixed outcome, may explain why their approach seems to be so different from yours. It may be that they are in the negotiation meeting for a different reason than you are.

Or there may be other factors at play ...

On the discussion forum Quora I asked the question: *How does the concept of negotiation differ in the Middle East from that in the West?* Below are extracts from three answers I received.

Currently in the Middle East, subjugating to someone else's demands is considered a weakness. Peace and compromise are not favored over honor and dignity.

The only difference I can see from practical application of the concept of negotiation is that in the Middle East, or the East in general, any conflict has an emotional deep perspective while in the West it depends solely on the given facts.

There is no difference. It only depends on the person you are talking to. In the end we are all human beings.

So three different opinions from three different speakers from the Arab world, but possibly all equally valid depending on who you happen to be negotiating with and what you are negotiating about.

In most non-Western cultures, people are interested in building up a relationship based on trust. This is why it's so common, for instance in Arab (see Section 5.2) and Central American countries, to do business with members of the family or with friends. This means that you should try to conduct your negotiation showing that you are trustworthy and that you have their objectives in mind, too.

A survey conducted among Asian and American businessmen asked the following question:

Imagine you are on a sinking boat with your wife, your mother, and your child, none of whom can swim. You can only save one of them. Which one?

The Americans were fairly well split between wives and children, 40 and 60 percent respectively, but all the Asians said they would save their mother. This has interesting implications. The family is something universal, but the importance we attach to each individual within that family may vary substantially. Thus in a negotiation, it's well worth finding out beforehand what your counterpart's priorities are likely to be so you will have more bargaining power without your counterpart feeling ripped off.

The key is not to mislead anybody: neither a business counterpart in your own country nor a person from another country. And then you find the common ground in the middle, and at a methodical pace you can make things work from there.

5.5 What is the best approach to managing differences?

One of the few undeniable differences in global business practice is that the world uses three dating systems. Europe uses the day/month/year system, China, Japan and Korea use y/m/d, and the United States uses m/d/y. Numbers also have different means of expression: in the Anglosphere there is a point after a whole number, whereas in Europe there is a comma. In India, numbers are based on the Vedic system, and a number such as 100,000 is written 1,00,000.

However apart from some culinary habits and other areas of life that do not impact on business, there are virtually no other cultural differences that are adopted en masse by an entire nation.

Cross cultural guides will tell you that our behavior and attitudes are influenced by our culture and that the way we use language is often a reflection of how we see the world and society. For instance, you can read that in many Australian aboriginal languages the word for *father and uncle is t*he same, whereas as in Finnish they even have separate words for the *son of one's daughter and* the *son of one's son. This* supposedly shows a difference in how families are viewed—the fewer the family words, supposedly the more close knit the family units are.

But such differences rarely prove very much and are often no more than interesting quirky factoids.

So what is the best approach to managing differences? Focus on the similarities. The reality is that we all have a lot more in common than we might imagine.

Tom Southern is an Englishman living in Australia who spent most of his working life as a top manager in a US company with a large office in Sidney. Much of his work involved dealing with Asia Pacific groups. He recalls:

Our overall aim was to focus on any aspects that would bring different cultures together, looking for small similarities and not worrying about things that were clearly quite different. However, one difficulty was that people make the immediate assumption that Americans and British are essentially very similar types of culture, types of business approach. So rather than understanding the similarities, the focus was on the differences, which might only be a relatively small percentage of the total picture. And both sides then start focusing on things that they find annoying or something that they feel we do better or that they do better. So bizarre as it may seem, I actually found there was more potential for conflict, with American businessmen than there probably was with any of our Asian partners.

Moral of the story: in meetings, negotiations, presentations or when socializing, initially look for the things you have in common, don't focus on the differences. Then when your relationship progresses you can move on to some of the differences, but without ever being negative or hinting that your way is the right way. Celebrate and learn from the differences.

I am not saying that cultural differences do not exist (see the end of Section 1.2), and that there are no differences in the way different nationalities conduct their business. Of course there are important differences—attitude to hierarchies (Section 1.10), attitudes to women (out of the scope of this book), level of formality (Section 2.3), face saving (Section 5.11), and negotiating styles—but such differences don't necessarily reflect the way every single person operates within a particular nationality or culture.

By only focusing on the differences, we lose sight of what we have in common.

5.6 How can I help non-natives take part effectively in a face-to-face meeting?

Forbes magazine once described meetings as "secret killers of productivity" and suggested they be simply banned, or held "only on Wednesdays"—all other decisions to be taken in absentia. A survey of 635 native English-speaking executives revealed that meetings are often ineffective for the following reasons: drifting off subject (83 percent of those surveyed complained of this issue), poor preparation (77 percent), not listening properly (68 percent), participants talking too much (62 percent), length (60 percent), and participants not talking enough (51 percent).

Many of the above factors will also impact on the effectiveness of a meeting for a non-native English speaker—but there are additional factors too.

As a native English speaker when you prepare for a meeting, you don't have to think about the kind of language you will have to use, what vocabulary and phrases you may need to learn, or any of the other issues that non-natives have to contend with. You can help non-natives by sending them an agenda with the list of points to be covered. This will enable them to do targeted preparation of exactly what they are going to say and what questions they may need to ask or answer.

So ensure that (1) there is an agenda, (2) everyone sticks to only what is on the agenda, and (3) any other business is deferred to a later time. The more you improvise with this structure or go off topic, the more difficulties your non-native counterparts will have.

However, not all meetings are arranged with an agenda. They may be informal, with a limited number of people who are:

- Reviewing what they've accomplished since the last meeting.
- Recounting the problems they've encountered that are keeping them from doing their job.
- Outlining what they will be working on until the next meeting or what they plan to do next and who is going to do it.

But just because there is no specific agenda, the overall structure of the meeting should nevertheless follow a pattern or a routine that a non-native could quickly become familiar with if he/she is going to be a regular participant. Again, what will throw off native speakers is if the meeting goes off course and other issues get discussed that are outside their own specific project or task. In such cases, non-natives will not have had a chance beforehand to prepare what they are going to say in terms both of content and the English language they will need to convey this concept. Non-natives will thus be at a disadvantage with respect to the other attendees.

To ensure the success of a meeting and thereby enhance the chances of a productive participation by non-native colleagues, try these strategies:

- Only say things that are relevant to everyone in the room.
- Enable one person to talk at a time, rather than various people talking over each other.
- Fix a time limit on the amount one person can say at one time—this should prevent participants from dominating and/or rambling.
- Discourage side conversations.
- Give eye contact to everyone, not just your native-speaking colleagues.
- Schedule regular breaks if the meeting is going to be long.

It also helps if you take time to summarize what has been discussed and decided. Do this frequently, preferably writing the points on the whiteboard—particularly numbers and dates (e.g., deadlines, delivery dates). This avoids problems later when one or more parties claim they hadn't understood.

Throughout the meeting, constantly reiterate what people have said—remember even if it was clear to you, it may not have been clear to other participants. This will entail you saying things like: "So what you're saying is ..." "If I understand you correctly, you think that ..." "I think what Mr. Hussein is saying is that ..."

If you have someone taking the minutes for you, get the person to project their screen so that participants can see the minutes as they are being taken. Again this will help to avoid misunderstandings.

And of course, you should also follow guidelines for speaking clearly and listening (see Chapter 3).

Finally, good meetings, whether formal or informal, require the chairperson (team leader, product/task owner, etc.) to set ground rules for how the meeting should be conducted. Such ground rules should always take into account the difficulties of non-native speakers.

5.7 What expressions, words, and grammar forms should I use in order to avoid confusing my non-native interlocutors?

Don't assume that just because a non-native speaker speaks and/or writes well that he/she can understand what you are saying orally. Often listening ability will be below speaking ability.

Non-natives may feel frustrated, stupid, and even humiliated if they don't understand you. They will likely attribute their lack of understanding to their own inadequacies rather than understanding that communication is a two-way process. This also means that they are reluctant to *admit* they don't understand, and thus lose face not only in front of you, but also in front of their colleagues.

So you need to do everything you can to facilitate communication. Your aim, as always, should be to inform your counterparts rather than confuse them.

The employees of the Delhi office of an international IT company told me they found their English counterparts in the London office difficult to understand when they used expressions such as *beat about the bush, one hell of a week,* and *come again?* (to ask for repetition). In some cases the problem is that the listener will try to find a literal interpretation (e.g., for *bush* and *hell*) and will not understand the use of *come* in a situation where it doesn't mean the opposite of *go*. Non-natives cannot be expected to deal with phrases such as *one throat to choke, punch the puppy, circle the wagon, blue sky thinking* and *ideas shower.* For more on the types of words and expressions to use and not use with non-natives, see Section 3.4.

The kind of grammatical constructions used in negotiations are typically conditionals, for example, *If you do this, I will do that. If I did that, would you do this?*

There is actually a subtle difference between those two examples, while the first indicates that I am quite sure of the situation and that it is quite likely to happen, the second is far more tentative. These differences may be lost on your non-native counterparts. If you feel that they may not be understanding, then break the bargaining down it a simpler format. You could say for example:

Possibility No. 1: We do x, you do y.

Possibility No. 2: You do x, we do y.

Let's talk about Possibility No. 1. On the basis that we do x, are you happy to do y? If you are not happy to do y, how can we help to convince you?

Also avoid grammatically complex expressions such as:

Were we to do XYZ ... Had we known this before ... Should you wish to ...

Instead keep it simple:

Another possibility is that we do XYZ.

We didn't know this. If we had known this, then ...

If you want to

Express yourself clearly, and check that you are being understood. Don't simply say "OK?," but say *So, does $10,000 seem a reasonable price?* or *So your cost would be $10,000, that's about 66,000 yuan—is that acceptable?*

Try to write down numbers and dates where possible, maybe simply on a note pad; or if several people are present, on a flip chart. There is frequent confusion between 15 and 50 or 16 and 60.

5.8 How can I ensure that meetings held via a conference call or tele-conference go well?

The average non-native attendees will probably understand the gist of what you say. They will thus lose many of the details. Your job is to ensure that they understood as much as possible. In some cases the gist may be enough, but if you are giving them instructions or explaining an intricate concept, then clearly you can't just cross your fingers and hope that they are understanding.

Other issues for non-native English speaking participants are:

- Native speakers dominating the meeting through their superior command of English;
- Native speakers not appreciating the necessity of non-natives occasionally talking in their own language amongst each other;

- Native speakers' lack of patience with the halting English of the non-natives;
- Non-natives possibly losing face in front of their compatriots due to poor command of English;
- Non-natives' reluctance to speak for fear of making mistakes in English.

An additional hurdle is that native-English speaking teams that have been together a long time are very hard for non-natives to deal with, as such teams all know each other well and tend to banter. If you all work for the same organization but in different offices around the world, you can help your non-native colleagues by:

- Providing opportunities for employees of different offices to meet face-to-face beforehand (even just by Skype), this really helps as they can picture each other, they are more familiar with accents, and they can joke and be more relaxed.
- Setting up a website of employees, with a photograph and a few personal and work details. This helps by enabling people to picture the people they are talking to and to know in advance what gender they are (this will help when trying to recognize who is who from the voices).

If you are the presenter, then it may be your job to take care of the technical side. This entails ensuring that:

- All participants have headsets and a microphone.
- Your screen is shared with all the attendees.
- People can hear you well and the sound quality in each office is acceptable.

On the next page are some tips that should help you improve the chances of successful audio and video conference calls (for additional tips see Section 3.8). You could email these ground rules to the native speaking participants in advance of the teleconference.

Ten Ground Rules for Teleconferences

1. Announce yourself each time you speak in a teleconference (if your voice is not already familiar to the others). Simply say: *Craig speaking. I think we ...*

2. When it is your turn to speak, point your mouth directly at the microphone. Even if you are close to the mike, but your mouth is pointing in another direction, it is still hard for those listening at the other end. Be aware that the sound quality of your counterparts' equipment may not be as high as it is at your end.

3. Never put your hand over your mouth while talking. Don't fiddle with things that are near the microphone or type on a keyboard, as this will distort the sound for your listeners.

4. Before answering a question, repeat the question so that everyone else can hear it.

5. Never assume that just because one non-native member on the call appears to understand everything, that all of his/her team members are also understanding. Try to direct questions at several members to ensure that everyone is following.

6. Members of some cultures tend to speak in a low voice as a form of deference to their interlocutors, or they may simply lack the confidence to speak in a loud clear voice. Mention the poor quality of your audio system as an excuse for asking them to speak louder.

7. Try not to talk when someone else is talking. If you need to interrupt, then do so by saying *Can I just interrupt* rather than just barging in.

8. People in the same room should avoid talking over each other and avoid side conversations that can be heard by all. And remember that laughing and in—jokes can be alienating for participants from other offices.

9. If there is likely to be a period of silence, for example because you need to confer with your colleagues that are sitting around you, then explain to your counterparts what is going on. So don't mute the phone without a prior explanation.

10. At the end of the conference call, go over again what has been discussed/decided, and email participants a summary.

Finally, it is worth finding out the latest developments in video and audio-conferencing. For instance, there is software that will eliminate the sound of clicking keys on a computer or repeatedly clicking a pen on and off.

5.9 What if my counterpart says something that I am not sure how to interpret?

Key to any communication, and particularly in meetings and negotiations, is checking that you have understood what your interlocutor has said and vice versa (see Section 3.9). An issue can arise when your non-native interlocutor appears to say two contradictory things in the same sentence. For instance you might say to your Chinese counterparts:

So delivery is not included in the charge?

And they reply:

Yes, delivery is not included.

You may not be sure which part of the sentence to give credence to: "yes" or "not." In reality, the Chinese person means *no, delivery is not included*—their use of *yes* is just dictated by what they would say in their own language. So if you spot an apparent contradiction, don't be afraid to seek clarification. In this case you could rephrase your question:

Delivery not included, correct?
So we have to pay extra for delivery, correct?
How much extra do we have to pay for delivery?

The third question will certainly ensure that you get confirmation about whether or not there is an extra fee for delivery.

Learning how to formulate clear questions that facilitate the non-native's capacity to provide you with the answer you were looking for is a key skill when dealing with non-native speakers.

5.10 What should I do if during a negotiation or meeting, the foreign party suddenly starts talking in their own language? Or if they stop talking completely and fall into silence?

Sometimes your foreign counterparts may suddenly start talking to each other in their own language without any explanation to you. This is completely normal, and important.

Rather than it being a sign of rudeness on their part, it is simply that they may need extra time to:

- Ensure that they have all understood what has been said
- Absorb and reflect on the progress of the meeting
- Check in with their other team members in order to reach some consensus as to their next move

Don't perceive their talking to each other as something negative. If you provide time for them to talk amongst themselves, you are actually likely to speed up the negotiation process. This is because they will have a much clearer idea from each other of what the options are, rather than just hearing them from you in a language that is not their own.

Your best approach is to tell them right at the beginning of the meeting that they should feel free to have mini discussions amongst themselves at any point they choose. This strategy reveals that you understand the difficulties they may have and that you acknowledge that in their culture taking team breaks is normal practice. You can also use these in-our-own-language pauses to enable your team to regroup.

Cross cultural expert Christalyn Brannen grew up in Japan and runs an international business consulting firm out of Berkley, California. In her excellent book *Going to Japan on Business*, she mentions another issue: your counterparts go completely silent for a "horrifying" 45 seconds. Christalyn writes that this maneuver can be interpreted in four different ways:

- It means nothing. They are simply taking *ma* ("time") silently
- It is a positive sign. They are impressed with what you have just said and are giving it a respectful *ma* ("space") before resuming.
- It is a negative sign. They are upset with what you just said and are trying to tell you so. They are also wondering why you don't understand this.
- They have read a cross-cultural book telling them silence makes foreigners, especially Americans, uncomfortable. They are aware of this and are trying to throw you off to force a concession.

Christalyn then reassures her readers that it will be immediately clear which of the four possibilities they are witnessing.

As mentioned many times, all cross cultural books risk stereotyping people and setting up misleading expectations. The Japanese you come across may not use silence as their secret weapon. However, such books might be worth reading for another purpose: to question your own approach to doing business. For instance, if the Japanese can use silence to good effect, then maybe you can. If the Arabs supposedly put a lot of stress on building up the social side of business, then maybe you could try doing the same and see if it benefits you.

5.11 What is "face saving?" How does this impact how people use English?

An Indian IT specialist was visiting his colleagues in Pisa, Italy, and was taken out for an Italian style coffee. The Italians noticed that every time the Indian took a tiny sip from his coffee, he then slipped a Mentos mint into his mouth. What was he up to? He was saving face—he hadn't wanted to offend them by refusing the coffee.

Saying "no" in some parts of Asia is a delicate affair and people will go to great pains to avoid giving a blunt refusal. They will say phrases such as: *I'm giving the matter my fullest consideration, but actually it's not possible,* or *conditions are a little bad.* In any case you should always try to give an excuse when you have to say no (*I have a meeting at that time,* etc.) and soften your refusal by saying what a pity, what a shame.

If you find that what your non-native partners apparently are doing is avoiding responsibility for their actions and being very indirect in what they say, then maybe what you are witnessing is face saving. In this case "face saving" means not putting other people in a "shameful" situation. The idea is always to try and keep a certain harmony, so individuals should never be singled out for either criticism or praise. This is in complete contrast to most western countries where we are used to criticizing and accepting responsibility, as well as receiving individual praise. Various everyday expressions underline this idea: *Give it to me straight. Put your cards on the table. Lay it on the line.*

Our preference for active forms (*we compared x with y* rather than *x was compared with y*) is indicative of this directness. We would say: *I'm really sorry but I had a little accident—I dropped my glass,* whereas speakers of other languages might say *I'm really sorry but it happened to me an accident—it fell from me the glass, as* if they had less control over the situation. Similarly in some African or Asian countries rather than saying *I missed the plane, they* might say *the plane left without me.*

So be aware that speakers of other languages may express themselves in a way that seems that they do not accept their responsibilities, though this may not be the case at all.

5.12 What else can I do to ensure that meetings and negotiations are effective for both the native and non-native speakers?

Non-natives are at a considerable disadvantage in a meeting or negotiation. This is primarily because of their lack of command of the English language (see Sections 1.7. 1.8, 3.3, 3.9). But there are also other actions you can take to help ensure the success of your meetings and negotiations:

- Listen carefully. Listen to what non-natives are really saying, rather than what you expect them to be saying.
- If you sense objection from your counterparts, think back to the last thing you said. Put yourself in their shoes, assess the possible reasons for the objection, and come up with some alternative proposals. Observe their reaction to your new proposals, and fine tune them until you find one that your counterparts go for.
- Make eye contact with everyone, not just with the most fluent speakers. The most fluent may not necessarily be the decision makers and may simply be the youngest members of the team and perhaps the lowest down in the hierarchy—thus addressing your remarks to them (rather than the more "important" people) could be seen as offensive.
- There is a tendency to look at those who are nodding—do not ignore those who are totally passive or are clearly in difficulty. Try to understand from them why they are unable to follow you.

- Be aware that your counterparts may have stereotypes of your country and possibly mistaken or unfounded opinions, just as you may have of them.
- Always remain calm. For some cultures, anger might be seen as a threat to harmony. If things don't seem to be going forward, then suggest reconvening later. Remember that the person you are dealing with may not be endowed with the same decision-making power that you have, and may thus have to refer back to their boss.
- If you sense a reluctance to close the deal, suggest that your counterparts take time to consider your offer. Give a realistic deadline and email/phone a few days before the deadline and say that if you have heard nothing from them in the next couple of days, you'll assume that they are not interested. You thus save them having to say "no" and it leaves both parties with their dignity and professionalism intact without blocking off future contact.

When the meeting is over, thank your counterparts. Reiterate your thanks through an email; or in the case of a very formal or important meeting, through a traditional letter sent on letterhead stationery.

Top Tips

- Prepare an agenda for the meeting in advance and send it to participants. Make sure all key words that are likely to be used during the meeting/negotiation, are also listed in the agenda. This will help your non-native counterparts in their preparations.
- In a negotiation, don't assume that your counterparts are participating for the same reasons as you are, nor that they necessarily have a final objective.
- Make sure all the participants know each other's names and positions.
- If one person in a non-native team speaks good English, don't assume that the rest of the team has the same level of English.

- Ensure you don't dominate a meeting or negotiation just because you are the most fluent. Never use your language power to your advantage.
- Ensure you have a clear idea of what you want to say before saying it—be specific, never vague.
- Use simple phrases.
- Find moments to repeat what you have said, and also what others have said. Constantly summarize what has been agreed. Do this both verbally and also in a written form on screen or on a whiteboard.
- Take breaks and get someone to type up what has been decided so far so that your counterpart has the opportunity to check that what both parties have said has been noted.
- Repeat back any questions that you are being asked. This will help the others to hear the question clearly, and you to check that you have understood the question.
- Unlike non-native speakers, you don't have to rack your brain for the right words or the correct grammatical constructions. So give the non-natives time to formulate their thoughts, and allow for moments of silence.
- Schedule moments when there can be a pause in the meeting, negotiation, or conference call so that the non-natives can talk to each other in their own language.
- Avoid participating in side conversations and making in-jokes with the native-speaking colleagues sitting next to you.
- Remember that communication works best when everyone is playing on the same level field and everyone has the same opportunity to play the ball.

CHAPTER 6

Presentations, Demos, Workshops, Seminars

Six things you didn't know you didn't know

- Microsoft PowerPoint was first introduced in 1987, and has an estimated 1.2 billion users worldwide. The phrase "Death By PowerPoint" seems to have been coined in the late 1990s by US army military personnel who were given a patch for their uniform for having "served and beyond the call of duty in making time consuming POWERPOINT presentations day after day, week after week, month after month without recognition."
- Around 350 PowerPoint presentations are started every second.
- There is far more training carried out in the Anglosphere than in other countries.
- Of the information the mind stores, 75 percent is received visually and only 13 percent through hearing, with the rest through taste and touch. Visual aids can improve learning by 200 percent and retention by 38 percent.
- TED presenters go through rigorous training before doing a presentation. This generally consists of a few practice runs via videoconference, where presenters are told how to stand, move, modulate their voice, move their head, and so on. They are also given a strict time limit and are encouraged not to improvise.
- Thomas Jefferson suggested that the "most valuable of all talents is that of never using two words when one will do."

For a more detailed discussion on how to present at conferences and congresses, see Chapter 19 in my book *English for Presentations at International Conferences* (Springer, 2nd ed., 2016). To learn how to conduct successful demos and training sessions, see *Presentations, Demos and Training Sessions: A guide to effective communication skills in English* (Springer, 2014).

Note: Unless specified otherwise, the term "presentation" is used in this chapter to cover presentations, demos, workshops and seminars, and all other occasions where one person is talking to a group of other people in order to train them or inform them why, when and how to take a particular action.

6.1 What are the key difficulties that non-native speakers have when attending presentations?

Whatever the audience, your presentation should be clear (both in terms of message, structure, language, and delivery), simple, and engaging.

However, it is not a given that non-natives will appreciate certain features that are typical of native-speaker presentations.

Slides

Recent TED presentations have virtually eliminated slides. However, for non-natives this makes listening to the presentation very hard work. They have only the words to go on. Non-natives need and appreciate slides—if they can't understand what you are saying, at least they can follow you through your slides.

Language

Non-natives are less likely to understand the subtleties and humor present in your speech—so keep these to a minimum. Avoid any slang or colloquial expressions. See Sections 2.7, 4.3, and 5.6.

Improvising and Winging

With non-natives you really need to choose your words carefully and keep your sentence structure simple. The moment you start deviating from your script and start *umming* and *ahing* and repeating yourself, you will lose a lot of non-natives who may not be able to keep up. Non-natives do not have the filtering mechanism of native speakers—for them every word and sentence potentially has equal importance, they are unable to differentiate between what is clearly an aside and what is a key point.

Sharing Personal Experiences, Informality

Some cultures are not used to self-disclosure or self-deprecation. They may find your anecdotes inappropriately personal, and may interpret deprecating remarks as being literal. Also they may be expecting a formal presentation, and informality on your part may be considered a sign of nonprofessionalism and will not be taken seriously.

Concentration Levels and Breaks

Non-natives' concentration is impeded by the fact that they have to make a double effort to understand what you are saying—not just the words themselves but what you are actually trying to say and its implications. Try to keep a presentation as short as possible; but if it has to be long, then schedule a couple of breaks.

6.2 How should I begin?

Start by introducing yourself—name, position, why you are doing this presentation (and what qualifies you to do it), what you know about your audience and their situation. The idea is that at this point you are not imparting key information, but just giving your audience time to get used to your voice and accent.

Your introduction should make everyone feel a bit more relaxed and thus less worried about not understanding you: reassure the audience that you will speak slowly and clearly.

At the beginning state clearly exactly what it is you are going to do by pointing to a skeleton of your presentation. This skeleton could also be self-standing (i.e., not necessarily on a slide), for example, on a whiteboard or flip chart. This tool helps you show your audience where you are in the presentation. Always make it clear when you are making a transition from one part of your presentation to the next—don't just say *now, moving on.* Instead, give them a clear indicator: raise your voice (particularly in an audio conference), use a different style of slide, take a few steps away from your laptop.

Whether you are presenting face to face or via a call, it helps if the participants not only have an agenda, but are also given info about any docs or files that they should have open or in front of them, any handouts that you plan to give them, whether they will be required to do any tasks, and whether the presentation will be available for them to download (either now or later).

Your audience will also certainly want to know when and how often breaks have been scheduled, what they should do if they don't understand (either the content or the way you speak), and when they can ask questions. Breaks also give non-natives an opportunity to speak to each other in their own language and compare what they have understood.

If your demo or presentation is being done via audio or videoconference, you may wish to set some ground rules about how participants should interact—see Section 5.8.

6.3 How can I help my audience understand me better?
Below are six tips for facilitating the level of comprehension of your audience.

1. Show slide, pause, then speak. Your audience may find it difficult to read and listen at the same time. So give them time to absorb the info on your slide, before you actually start speaking about it. Use your voice and your cursor to highlight the important info. But move your cursor slowly.
2. Speak slowly, articulate clearly, and pause often. While you are talking, underline what you are saying with hand gestures, for example, you say "sales have been increasing rapidly" use an upward movement of your hand and arm. Ensure that you explain the meaning of any key words.
3. Have two versions of your presentation—use one as a handout. You can email your presentation (not just the slides, but a full text of what

you plan to say) to participants in advance. If not, at least provide a summary, preferably translated into their own language. By having a handout in advance, for example, a print out of the slides but containing extra text or notes, they will be able to follow you much better during the live presentation. If you decide not to use a handout, then another option is to send them the slides after you have done the presentation. However, these slides could be much more detailed than the slides you showed, for example, more text, more detailed diagrams, and additional slides. If you are doing a product/service presentation, have the technical details of your product and service translated into their language.

4. Given the language difficulty, some of your audience may get lost. Number your slides (the audience can follow/find them easily in the handout) and refer back to the agenda to indicate where you are in the presentation.

5. Don't overload your audience with information. Experts recommend having three key points. This is particularly true for non-native audiences whose levels of concentration and comprehension may well be impeded by having to listen in a language that is not their mother tongue.

6. Make frequent summaries. Don't worry about saying the same thing more than once. Summaries give audiences a chance to rehear what they might have missed earlier or not completely understood.

6.4 How much will my accent and level of formality impact on their understanding of my presentation?

In addition to the six tips given in 6.3, you need to be aware of the effect that your accent will have on your listener's ability to understand you. Researcher Ravindra P. Jumde from India told me:

I have attended many international conferences and meetings with collaborators. I have witnessed first hand the difficulty that audiences have in understanding the English pronunciation of Indian researchers.

If you have ever listened to Indians, Pakistanis, and Bangladeshis speaking you may have noticed that, for instance, they use a *v* sound where an American or Brit would use a *w*, for example, *vest* versus *west*; that there are some idiosyncrasies in their vocabulary and grammar, and that they tend to write and speak in a more formal way.

Likewise, there are sounds that may be unique to your own accent. For example, a non-native may have difficulty if you say *ting* for *thing*, or *fink* for *think*, or *twenny* for *twenty*.

A strong accent from anywhere—South Carolina, Maine, New York, Belfast, Glasgow, East London—is likely to cause difficulties for a non-native. Of course what is "'strong" is very much subjective and really depends on the amount of exposure the members of your audience have had to your particular accent.

Essentially you need to be aware of what difficulties your accent may cause (see Section 3.4). Being aware of such differences will help you not only in your dealings with non-native English speakers, but also with native English speakers from other parts of the globe—not only in presentations, but also in all interactions.

Whatever your accent, try to speak slowly and enunciate words very clearly.

Another related issue is the level of formality that you use. Choudhury Abul Anam Rashed, a PhD student in engineering, commented:

> As an international student of Engineering, I have noticed that my English differs from native English speakers. Like other Bangladeshi students, the medium of instruction at an undergraduate level was English. But the English we used seems rather more formal than is used, for example, in the West. On some occasions I believe that my high level of formality in English may have been misinterpreted.

So just as Choudhury's use of very formal English may have made him seem too distant in the eyes of his Anglosphere audience, if you adopt a very informal style this may be perceived as being superficial or unprofessional for an audience that is used to a more formal approach.

6.5 How should I speak? What kind of language should I use?

One of the best presentations I have ever seen a native speaker give to a non-native audience was a speech given by Don Daughters, then worldwide manager of IBM, to an SME partner company in Italy. He spoke slowly and clearly, with no slides at all, and with an incredible enthusiasm and will to communicate his message. Everyone in his audience, including those with low level English, was able to understand him—what they might have missed from the language was made up for by his tone of voice and body language.

This is how he began:

> I'm absolutely thrilled, excited to be here. You have a superb, exciting market place. You have an incredible product. You have leading edge technology in this product that would rival anything that I have ever seen in the world. So that's why I'm here, that's why I'm excited.

> Let me tell you about this market. Small business is big business. There are 74 million small businesses around the world. 71 million of those businesses have less than 15 employees. They will spend $168 million next year. That's a lot of money. Now, if you think those numbers are big, in this beautiful country of yours you have 1.8 million small businesses and they will spend six billion dollars next year.

What can we learn from this speech?

- The vocabulary he uses can be understood even by someone with only a fairly rudimentary knowledge of English.
- His average sentence length is 9.2 words, his longest sentence is 29 words.
- This short sentence length means that he can pause naturally many times. This prevents him from speaking too quickly,

and allows his audience to have time to mentally translate and absorb what he is saying.

- Every sentence moves logically into the next.
- He repeats his concepts. He uses one word (e.g., *thrilled*) and then uses a synonym (*excited*)—if his audience didn't catch *thrilled* then they will catch *excited*.
- He summarizes: *So that's why I'm here, that's why I'm excited.*
- He introduces a new topic with a short sentence that introduces the key word: *Let me tell you about this market.*
- He presents numbers in a simple way.

Daughters had prepared a written version of his speech. By preparing a written version, he was able to create short sentences and weed out any dross. Daughters stuck to his script, which meant there was no improvisation, no umming and ahhing, no going off at a tangent. This meant that he took his audience with him so they could follow his every word.

By having a script, he was also able to practice it until it came out of his mouth perfectly.

Daughters traveled the world giving speeches like this. His formula for speaking was tried and tested, and it works. I strongly suggest you adopt a similar style. However, in most cases it would be worth having slides so that those with little or no English can still follow you.

6.6 How much text should I have in my slides? How visual should they be?

Normally we are taught that less is more, that we should put the bare minimum number of words in our slides. This is true for an audience with a reasonably high level of English.

But with an audience whose English is quite poor, the more written words you give them the more they will understand you—remember that reading is at least 20 times easier than listening. This doesn't mean cramming your slides with text as this will obviously make them unreadable. What it does mean is possibly having a greater number of slides to accommodate the extra text you will need.

But don't adopt a karaoke style of reading your slides aloud. If you have too much text, then your presentation could probably just be emailed to the participants.

Instead, show the slide, let the audience read the text, and then interpret the text for them. By "interpret" I mean explain key words or concepts, highlight the importance, suggest the implications, and so on. And don't feel you have to explain all the text; just focus on those bits of the text that you think are the most important or that will be the most interesting for the audience.

If you are speaking in English to an audience that does not understand English at all (or only very little), that is, there are simultaneous interpreters present, then the more visual the better. You will considerably simplify the life of the translators and the audience if you use very visual slides. Your slides then just become signposts that help the audience understand what their interpreter is saying.

6.7 How can I check that the audience is following me when I am doing a demo or training session?

When doing a demo or training session, clearly the most important factor is that the audience can understand and follow you. Strategies that may work with a native audience will not necessarily work with a non-native audience.

Questions such as *OK? Is that clear? Is everybody following me?* are likely to be met with a nod of the head, and offers such as *Please interrupt me if you want me to go over something again?* are likely to be ignored. This may be the result of several factors:

1. In some cultures it may be considered rude to interrupt.
2. They may be embarrassed that they haven't understood something that they think they should have understood.
3. They may think their colleagues have understood and therefore not want to show themselves up.

So you have to assume that they won't understand quite a lot of what you say. To improve their understanding:

- Have clear slides where they can read/see what you've said;
- Summarize frequently using different words;
- Make your session as interactive as possible—if only you do the talking, you will never know how much the audience is taking on board;
- Ask attendees to make summaries (verbal, or via email—see the end of this subsection) of what they have understood so far;
- Occasionally stop and ask what the attendees think are the most important things they've learned to so far.

The last two points work well because you are not asking specific questions where an attendee might lose face. You will also get feedback to enable you to decide what parts of your demo/training you need to go over again.

More than you would do with native speakers, with non-natives you really need to check their body language as an indicator of whether they are following or not. For example, many Indians put more emphasis on body language and their facial expression than we do, and they expect the presenter to see from their face that they want to ask a question. So in a training session, the Indian audience may not ask questions of their own accord but will need to be prompted by you.

Schedule moments when you ask participants to write down the questions that they would like to ask. They can either then discuss these questions in their own language with each other, or ask you directly. If your session is via audio or videoconference, then such questions can simply be emailed or messaged to you. Again, this strategy removes any sense of losing face for your audience.

6.8 What do I need to be aware of if I am doing my session by audio conference or videoconference?

In an audio conference, you lose all visual clues from the audience: are they following you or are they on their cell phone? Are they leaning forward or raising their hand because they want to ask a question? Do they looked interested or bored? Likewise their comprehension of what you are saying is impeded by their not being able to interpret your body language or see your hands when you make a point. Obviously, in a videoconference these issues are less serious; but unless the visual quality is very high, your mouth movements may not even be visible to your audience.

If you combine the above with the fact that the audience will typically be very passive and thus be concentrating much less than in a face-to-face session, you really need to take action. Imagine listening over the phone to someone talking in Spanish or French for an hour—you would need to be massively motivated not to nod off after a while.

So first consider whether what you want to say could be better expressed through a written document or via a recorded visual presentation that participants could watch at their leisure.

If you must use an audio or videoconference then it is essential to:

- Send documentation in advance of your session—this could include slides that the audience can follow while you are talking.
- Add an interactive element—set tasks for them to do; integrate frequent mini Q&A sessions.
- Schedule lots of breaks during which they can relax a bit, chat with other participants in their own language, or send you messages with questions that they would like you to discuss.

An obvious but crucial element is that the sound quality must be high. Attendees should listen with headphones rather than using speaker phone. In any case, before you start you need to check that everyone can hear (see) you clearly.

6.9 How should I end my presentation?

It is unlikely at the end of your presentation that a non-native audience will have understood everything you have said. This may not matter at a product/service presentation. But if you have been giving a demo or a training session, your audience needs to feel that you are available if they have any questions and doubts.

A way to reassure audiences is to finish with a series of 2 to 3 slides in which you:

- Provide a summary;
- Provide a handout if you haven't already done so;
- Indicate where they can download your presentation;
- Tell them where they can find further information;
- Give them your email address if they have any further questions to ask;
- Tell them what your immediate schedule is, and whether you have time available now to talk to them.

If you have been watching someone else's presentation, and at the end of their presentation you want to ask a question, make sure you phrase it as simply as possible and enunciate loud and clear. One of the things foreign presenters dread the most about giving a presentation is not being able to understand the questions from the audience—be sensitive to this and consider whether it might not be easier for both parties if you simply asked your questions after the presentation (e.g., in the coffee break or over a meal).

If you are at a workshop or seminar, make sure you don't just talk to the other native speakers; and never use your linguistic superiority to dominate any discussions.

Finally, remember that you can understand and react much more quickly than a non-native. So give the others time to collect their thoughts and mentally prepare what they want to say.

Top Tips

- Most audiences of whatever nationality tend to appreciate the following: relatively informal delivery but with genuine enthusiasm, a narrative style, clarity and simplicity of expression, attractive slides without excessive text, not too much detail, minimal theory and lots of examples, and feeling involved.

- Where possible, present your information visually rather than verbally.
- Speak slowly, articulate clearly, and pause often. Use easy-to-understand, clear English.
- Use gestures to explain and emphasize your points.
- Have a clear storyboard/skeleton/route map for your audience to follow, and refer to it often throughout the presentation.
- Exercises, tasks, and demos take much longer to set up with a non-native audience, so you are likely to achieve much less in a session than you would with native speakers.
- Non-native speakers will often blame themselves for not understanding, attributing their lack of understanding to a lack of command of the English language—it's your job to make your English comprehensible to them. If you do, your audience will listen much more attentively and you will massively improve all future relationships with them.
- Those of other cultures may expect you to know your product and service inside out and to be able to describe it in precise detail without giving approximations with regard to size, weight, price, and so on.

CHAPTER 7

Translating and Interpreting

Seven things you didn't know you didn't know

- Translators and interpreters used by the military, for example, in Iraq, Afghanistan, often become regarded as potential traitors as they may appear to have a split allegiance. In Guantanamo Bay, some translators/interpreters were even charged as being Al Qaeda infiltrators.
- When a hospital interpreter translated the Spanish *intoxicado* (meaning suffering from food poisoning) as *intoxicated*, the doctors treated the patient as if he had taken a drug overdose. The patient was left with permanent quadriplegia, and the malpractice apparently cost the hospital $71 million in compensation.
- Donald Trump's disjointed syntax, run-on sentences, and limited vocabulary pose an ethical dilemma for simultaneous translators. If translators report what Trump actually says and how he says it, then listeners may struggle to understand. According to one translator, if Trump's words were rendered into smoother intelligible speech this might make him sound like "an ordinary politician who speaks properly."
- According to Pope Francis, the phrase "lead us not into temptation" in the Lord's prayer is not a good translation. Instead, the French version—do not allow me to fall into temptation—highlights that temptation is Satan's department.
- In November 2010, an Italian national newspaper reported that Google Translate had translated *Io non ho votato Berlusconi* with "I voted for Berlusconi." And not just when translating into English, but into any language. It is believed by some that this was not an error, but that the program had been deliberately tampered with to obtain that result.

- In 1985, Ronald Reagan deliberately misled the public when he falsely claimed: "I'm no linguist but I have been told that in the Russian language there isn't even a word for freedom."
- The Japanese breed of dog *Shih Tzu* is pronounced without the *t* by many prudish British dog-owners.

7.1 From a translator's point of view, what kind of issues are involved when translating?

A frequently cited issue of the problems connected with translating is the naming a product or service that is going to be marketed internationally. For example, Diet Coke had to be changed to "Coca-Cola Light" in some countries due to negative connotation of the word "diet." Foreign companies have also had to adapt their names to English-speaking markets: Marcel Bich dropped the "h" from his name when branding pens outside France, and Perrier's soft drink *Pschitt* obviously had to be renamed. Choosing the right word is thus a key element to translating, particularly when more than one is available, or in cases where no equivalent word exists in the target language.

Everyday factors that translators have to think about are:

- How well written the original is, whether they are going to have to "rewrite" parts to make it more comprehensible, and whether they think some words or phrases are so totally redundant that they are not worth translating;
- Level of formality;
- Level of technical knowledge of the reader;
- Number of hours/days the translation will take.

These factors should be considered when you assign a document for translation. It might be worth reviewing your document to look for potential translation issues, and if necessary sending some instructions to the translator to give him/her an idea of the kind of tone/formality and readership you are targeting.

It is important that you see translations as a two-way task. There should be a dialog between you and the translator, where the translator feels free to contact you for explanations.

Translators are not specialists in every field, and there is bound to be terminology that they are not familiar with. Thus for important documents, it is imperative that you have them checked by someone who knows both languages (and the topic) very well.

7.2 How can I judge whether a translator and a translation are of good quality?

If you were a lawyer and needed the services of an accountant, you wouldn't contact the first accountant that you found on Google—you would probably ask friends and colleagues for recommendations, or failing that you would ask the accountant for references.

Yet for many people, including many professionals, translators seem to be afforded a wizard status. You just assume that because someone has a Spanish-sounding surname and speaks impeccable English that he/she can also translate totally accurately between the two languages. Not so. Translation is an art and requires years, if not decades, of experience.

Translators can do massive damage with poor translations. They also tend to be underpaid. However, the amount they charge is to some extent an indication of the quality of the service they are offering—in the same way as a doctor, lawyer, or accountant.

I suggest that if your company or institute has an important doc to translate, you don't just put it out to tender and choose the cheapest offer; instead, ask each contender to provide a translated page or two of your document, and then get an expert to judge whose is the best translation. Also make sure that the mother tongue of your translator is the language that is being translated into ... and get plenty of references. There are a lot of cowboy translators out there!

7.3 How can I improve the chances that my document is clear and easy to read and will thus be translated accurately?

Charles Babbage was the inventor of the first programmable computing device. In his memoirs, he claimed that he twice had been asked the question: "Pray, Mr. Babbage, if you put into the machine wrong figures, will the right answers come out?" If Babbage had been alive today, he would have used the IT expression GIGO (garbage in garbage out).

The same applies to a translation—a poorly written document in English will become a very poorly written or incomprehensible document when translated into another language.

So before you submit your doc to translation, it might be worthwhile following these ten guidelines. Note: Many of these are covered in more detail in Chapter 4.

Ten Ways to Make Your Documents More Translatable

1. Remove everything that is not strictly necessary. Most docs can be reduced by about 25 percent with no real loss of content.
2. Clarify anything that doesn't make sense—it will make even less sense when translated. The process of translation will uncover all the unrecognized/unresolved problems of the original. A good translator also has to be a good editor.
3. Ensure that each sentence only expresses one idea.
4. Use active (e.g., *we did x*) rather than passive sentences (*x was done*). The advantage of an active sentence is that it must contain a subject, and this subject must precede the verb (in English). This means that the translator (human or automatic) is likely to produce a more accurate translation.
5. Don't use synonyms for key words. If your key word is "user," don't use *operator, technician, utilizer, webmaster* or *end user* to mean the same thing. Stick to *user* throughout. *You* know that they are all synonyms, but the translator (human or automatic) cannot know, and nor can your readers.
6. Avoid uncommon nontechnical words (e.g., *ballyhoo, bedraggled, bedlam*), slang (e.g., *ten bucks*), and idiomatic expressions (e.g., *the ball is in your court*).
7. If a sentence is very long (more than 30 words) or contains a lot of punctuation, divide up the sentence into shorter sentences.
8. Replace pronouns and forms such as *it, they, which, the former, the latter* with the key words that they refer to. This avoids the translator having to decide which previous word *it* or *they*, for instance, refers to.

9. Look out for any ambiguous phrases (*I left her there to pay the bill*—who paid: me or her?). Because you are the author of your doc, and thoroughly understand the topic and have become very familiar with your own text, you may not notice such phrases. So a good idea is to let someone else check it, too.

10. Ensure that you use punctuation correctly—a misplaced comma or lack of a hyphen can change the meaning of a sentence (e.g., *I saw a man eating shark* vs. *a man-eating shark*), and thus the translated version of that sentence.

These ten guidelines are really just rules for writing in general. If you apply them rigorously to docs that are to be translated, you will massively help the translator (human or automatic) to understand your text and will thus get a more accurate translation.

7.4 How good is Google Translate and other automatic translators?
Few technologies attract such contrasting opinions as Google Translate (GT). Here are four of the most common opinions:

1. From a person who has no knowledge of languages at all and imagines that GT does exactly what it says on the tin: *I can translate my document into French simply by inserting my English text into GT and pressing the "French" button. The resulting document will be in French. C'est facile!*

2. From a person who is not a professional translator and sees the result of a document translated from French (or whatever language) into English: *This is preposterous. There are parts that make absolutely no sense. I will never ever use GT.*

3. From a professional translator and purist: *GT makes a lot of mistakes. I can do a better much better job than GT. I would never use GT. It is a waste of my time.*

4. From a translator who is a practical timesaver: *GT is not perfect, but for reasonably technical jobs it provides a first draft that is around 75 to 80 percent correct, which I can then revise myself. With a little experience of knowing how to work efficiently with GT the whole process is considerably quicker than if I started from scratch.*

The first opinion is clearly wrong—GT is not some miracle cure, you have to have the knowledge to be able to correct the resulting document. The second and third opinions are very common, but are mistaken given the fact that the fourth opinion is, in fact, the closest to reality.

I used Google Translate (GT) to translate the following text from Turkish (a language I don't know at all) into English. The text is part of a newsletter sent by a Turkish company which brings together English-speaking teachers with students who want to practice their oral English.

> 80 percent of all content on the Internet is written in English, 400 million people speak English as mother tongue, 700 million people speak English as second language, in our country, 99.2 percent of the students see English at school.
>
> Since almost all of the students are taking English lessons, what little, young, and adult do not speak English? We can hold the state, the circulation, the economic situation, the educational system and the geography responsible for this. We can develop hundreds of ideas on the answer to this question, but instead of filling ourselves with negative thoughts, we can search for the answer to how we can overcome this problem, open a brand new page, and improve our English.
>
> We can no longer have no ink.

Things to note:

- GT's translations are a bit like a parson's egg: you will find parts that are very good (e.g., *80% of all content on the Internet is written in English*), parts that are clearly wrong but which are nevertheless decipherable (e.g., *99.2% of the students see English*), and parts that apparently make no sense at all (e.g., *We can no longer have no ink.*). This is because GT searches for existing translations—the statistic about Internet content is very common, whereas the percentage of Turks learning English at school is not common at all and thus may never have been translated by anyone before.

- When you use GT to translate a document from English into another language, bear in mind that it might look something like the Turkish text above. Don't be mesmerized by seeing your text in a foreign language and assume that you have miraculously achieved an accurate translation. GT does a pretty good job (only about 10 to 15 percent of the Turkish text is incorrect), but it does need revision and editing.
- GT does not translate each language with the same accuracy. Given that Spanish is spoken by 400 million people and Turkish by around 70 million people, GT's English-Spanish-English service is used far more than the Turkish one. It can draw on more documents and examples, and is thus generally more accurate. Spanish was also one of the first languages Google used to test its automatic translations on. Mandarin Chinese (nearly one billion speakers) was introduced by Google much later, and the accuracy of the translations is lower, also as a consequence of the fact that Chinese, unlike Spanish, is much further from English from a structural and vocabulary point of view.

The translation *We can no longer have no ink* is classic Google Translate, and is the reason why in some circles GT has a bad reputation. In reality the phrase means: *No longer without English*, which was the title of the newsletter. GT's confusion with *ink* is inexplicable according to a Turkish colleague of mine. Interestingly, Bing translates the phrase as *No more English*, which although closer to the original is totally misleading.

In Google's defense I would like to make three important points.

1. When GT makes a mistake—very often the mistake is glaringly obvious, and is thus easy to spot (unlike the insidious mistakes that humans often make).
2. GT makes no claims to do a perfect job, only that its service is improving day by day (which I can guarantee it is). No humans do a translation without checking it over, so you need to check very carefully every GT you do.

3. It takes GT a few seconds to translate thousands of words. I pitted Italian PhD students against GT, to translate a short and relatively easy paragraph from Italian into English. The students took around six minutes to translate it, and then a few more minutes to correct it. GT took six seconds and there were no more mistakes in it than in the students' final version. Obviously, a native-speaking English person who was fluent in Italian, would have made fewer mistakes. But at the end of the day, using GT as a draft (requiring further revisions) is a much quicker option than starting a translation from scratch.

Moral of the story: Get over the fact that Google Translate makes some ridiculous mistakes. This is not a sign that GT is incompetent, just that it is still a relatively immature technology.

And don't forget that humans are just as a capable of making terrible mistakes. In 1988, the California travel agency Banner Travel Services published an advertisement in the local yellow pages that offered travel packages to exotic destinations. But instead of *exotic* they wrote *erotic*—a typo that reputedly lost them about 80 percent of their customers. Google Translate doesn't make typos.

7.5 What do I need to be careful about when translating the names of products and services into another language?

There are hundreds of examples of poorly translated names of products or slogans on the Internet. Many of these are urban tales, such as the classic Chevrolet Nova which apparently didn't sell in Spanish-speaking countries because *no va* means *it doesn't go* (in reality the Nova sold very well, particularly in Venezuela).

However, there are certainly cases where translations have gone very wrong. Thus careful thought needs to go into such slogans, including the option of not translating at all but using a different slogan. In Raymond Ng's book *Customers from Afar*, this issue is explained by a manager of a telecommunications company in Vancouver that was targeting Chinese customers who wished to communicate with family and friends back home.

We have a long-distance package called *Real Plus* that is meant for every one of our customers, but the name was no good for our Chinese customers because the direct translation of "Real Plus" in Chinese means "sure increase (in fees)." We wanted a name that could address their family ties and the need to make frequent long-distance calls. So we stayed away from direct translation and adopted the Chinese saying "One Family Across the Distance" as the name of our package.

You will generally have three options for translating to another language, the easiest of which is the first one listed below, but the most effective maybe the third.

1. Leave the name of your product in English—however ensure that it doesn't have a strange meaning or "vulgar" sound in the other language. Apparently Ford was unaware that Pinto in Brazilian Portuguese means "tiny male genitals," and Vicks introduced its cough drops into the German market without realizing that the German pronunciation of "v" is "f" making "Vicks" slang for sexual intercourse.

2. Change the name of the product depending on the country—for the German market, Mars Inc. changed the name of their chocolate bar to Raider, as Twix has a similar sound to *Wichsen* (to masturbate).

3. Begin from scratch with a new version coined directly in or for the language of the country/target market. This can be a complete phrase (as in the Chinese *One Family Across the Distance*) or can simply be a change of spelling that is more suitable for a particular country/market/language. For example, one of Unilever's cleaning products is called *Vim, Jif, Cif, Viss,* and *Handy Andy* depending on which of its 51 markets it is sold in.

The same rationale is also applicable to nonbranded items, for example, the titles of public health pamphlets, book and movie titles, names and acronyms of institutes, and every other imaginable case where something needs "converting" into another language.

7.6 I am planning to use an interpreter. What do I need to look out for?

In an article for the *New York Times* entitled *In Afghanistan, Humor Finds Its Way in Lost Translation*, Eileen Guo recounts various episodes that highlight how important it is to enunciate words clearly when speaking through an interpreter. In one episode, a US military trainer was asking an Afghan government official about some new computers that had been installed. He asked *How's the system?* which was translated as *How's your sister?* In another case, a foreman instructing some local laborers, said: *tell them to get their shovels and start working. I will be back in an hour.* This was translated as *go shower and come back in an hour.*

In both cases the interpreters were clearly struggling with the American accent. So a key rule when speaking to non-natives and especially when using an interpreter is to enunciate each word clearly. Below are a few points you should bear in mind.

Guidelines for Using an Interpreter

1. Engage a competent interpreter and brief him/her beforehand on what you are going to say. If possible send the interpreter a written document with the exact words you will be saying. The interpreter can then prepare the translation in advance.
2. Learn about your audience—their culture, their communication style. This should help you in the pace of delivering what you want to say and in being aware of your body language. It should also strengthen your ability to interpret their facial reactions to what you are saying.
3. It is much easier for the interpreter if you speak and then he/she translates (i.e., consecutive interpreting), rather than you speaking and them translating at the same time (i.e., simultaneous translation). Be aware that the interpreter may require more words than you used in order to communicate the message effectively.
4. Your interpreter may not be a professional interpreter, but just a local person who also happens to speak English. Ensure that the person understands that the job is to interpret what you say,

rather than join in on the conversation. Go easy on the interpreter, but at the same time be constantly on the lookout for signs of hesitation when the interpreter is translating, followed by signs of surprise on the faces of the listeners. The combination of these two signs means that some kind of mistranslation may have taken place.

5. If you are using an interpreter for a presentation or in a formal meeting, then consider cutting what you would have to say by about half.

6. Although some experts recommend making eye contact exclusively with the person you are speaking to rather than the interpreter, this can be demeaning for the interpreter. Instead, make eye contact with the interpreter when you begin a new sentence, but then turn immediately to your interlocutor.

7. Begin with a bit of small talk to allow the interpreter to warm up.

8. Talk slowly and in short sentences. An interpreter cannot remember a series of long sentences. Give the interpreter time to mentally translate your sentence before uttering it to the audience.

9. Write down any numbers and dates—different cultures use different numbering and date systems, so there is room for mistranslation.

10. Don't ask multiple questions. Just ask one question at a time, otherwise the interpreter may forget to ask one of the multiple questions. Also, keep your questions as short as possible.

11. Use as few words as possible, with each sentence expressing a single thought. If that doesn't work, try saying the same things twice but in different ways. This ensures a greater chance of your message being translated correctly.

12. Make periodic summaries. This helps the interpreter check that he/she has been translating correctly, and it gives the listener(s) a second chance to absorb the information.

13. Don't let the interpreter take over. It is not their role to conduct the session.

14. Interpreting is tiring and stressful, so allow for short breaks every 10 to 15 minutes.

My favorite episode from Afghanistan that Eileen Guo recounts is this, which according to her article, is not the only time the same "mistake" has been made:

> One day, the New Zealand Provincial Reconstruction Team had lunch with some local village elders. At the end of the meal, they wanted to thank their hosts. One of them spoke on behalf of the team, saying: "Thank you for your great hospitality. The food was delicious." But the interpreter was confused. He translated: "Thank you for your great food. We will build you a hospital."

Interpreting is a big issue. A report from the UK showed that a third of police forces are using "unqualified" interpreters to conduct crucial interviews with foreign suspects. In one case, the services of a retired priest were used to interpret for a Portuguese-speaking man from Guinea Bissau, in west Africa, who was accused of sexual offenses. The priest struggled to communicate with the suspect due to his poor knowledge of Portuguese and his refusal to translate the sexual terms. The case of the priest comes from a dossier compiled by Professor Guillermo Makin, a Spanish translator, who also stated that:

> There have been cases where interpreters were making up answers because they did not understand what was being said to them. We don't know what else might have gone wrong in courts and police interviews because obviously no one else knows what is being said.

Top Tips When Using a Translator

- Aim to produce translated documents that are of the same standard as you would expect from a document written in English. You and your department/institute/company are no less responsible when you write in another language than when you write in English.
- You can considerably help the translator by providing him/her with a doc that is easily translatable: simple, no redundancy, short sentences, no ambiguity, clear structure, no typos, and so on.

- When you receive a doc that has been translated into English by a foreign counterpart, don't automatically associate a poor translation with incompetency or inefficiency.
- Don't be cynical about automatic translation software. These programs are getting better and better every day. If you dismissed them last year as being unreliable, you may find that this year they have improved massively.
- When using an interpreter, if you realize that your counterpart can understand English after all, do not bring this to his/her attention. Continue with the interpretation process unless the counterpart decides to speak directly to you.
- Translating your company's brochures and websites accurately is likely to lead to higher sales. A survey found that nearly three quarters of people prefer to buy a product or service that is provided with information in their own language, and half said that the ability to obtain info in their own language was more important than the price in affecting their likelihood of purchase.
- Studies have revealed similar levels of stress for simultaneous interpreters and air traffic controllers. So go easy on your interpreter.
- The quality of a translated document that you receive from a foreign client may be inconsistent. A single document may not have all been translated by the same person, and parts of other previously translated documents may have been incorporated. This can lead to different styles and formats being used within the same doc, thus giving it a nonprofessional appearance, and facilitating the chances of apparent non sequiturs due to cut and pastes that ended up in the wrong place.
- Be aware of the consequences that mistranslation can cause. For example, a 1905 treaty between Russia and Japan was drafted in English and French (the languages of international law). In a clause relating to the inspection of territories, the French version used the verb *contrôler* (check, inspect, verify) whereas the English version used the much more threatening word *control*. So use someone really qualified to go through any important documents that you may have had translated.

CHAPTER 8

Socializing

Seven things you didn't know you didn't know

- In the late 1730s, a Swiss travel writer commented that it was "almost dangerous for a well-dressed foreigner to walk the streets of London, for he ran a great risk of being insulted by the vulgar populace, the most cursed brood in existence. He is sure of not only being jeered at and bespattered with mud, but as likely as not dead cats and dogs will be thrown at him."
- The Japanese word for "four" also means "death," and in Japan they have no fourth floors in hotels and they never give four of something as a present. Many hotels in the West do not have a 13th floor, and there are often no number 13 seat rows in airplanes.
- We say *mom and dad* (but *brothers and sisters*), the Chinese say *dad and mom*. We say *black and white*, but half the world says *white and black*.
- Czechs, and several other European groups, frequently use functional or academic titles instead of names: *Mr. mayor, Mr. caretaker, Mr. engineer*, and so on.
- English has no equivalent for some foreign words. For example, the German word *schadenfreude* means the pleasure derived by someone from another person's misfortune. The term *ronin* means a "masterless samurai" in Japanese, a student who fails their college entrance examination and then spends the next year restudying to try for a second time.
- Uglish (a mix of Uganda and English) contains words that standard English could clearly benefit from: *beep*—to call someone once and hang up before they pick up; *buffalo*—someone who uses incorrect or inarticulate English words, *bullet*—a leaked exam paper, *side dish*—somebody's mistress.

- A pre-US 2016 election cover of Britain's satirical weekly magazine, *Private Eye*, showed Trump pointing his fingers to his head like a gun, with the line "Vote Trump, it's a no brainer." Trump then tweeted the post, commenting "British media gets behind me."

8.1 What strategies can I adopt to ensure an effective conversation with my non-native colleagues?

A good way to ensure that both parties have their fair share of a conversation is to adopt a ping-pong approach:

1. I say something.
2. You comment on what I have said, encouraging me to say a little more.
3. I say a little more and then turn the conversation over to you by asking you a question related to what I have just been talking about.
4. You say your piece.
5. I comment on your piece and encourage you to continue (as you did in Step 2).
6. You do what I did in Step 3 and so on.

No player has the ball for very long—each player participates equally and is equally responsible for a good rally. Of course, there are plenty of American and Brits who don't have ping-pong conversations. In *The Pursuit of Attention*, sociologist Charles Derber reported the results of a study done on face-to-face interactions. His researchers noted which participants competed for attention. Their results showed that often without even being conscious of it, we try to turn the attention of others to ourselves. This is illustrated by the following exchange:

Sam: I've signed up for a course on mindfulness.
Pat: I'm thinking of getting into mindfulness too.
Sam: Really?
Pat: Yes my brain is constantly getting cluttered up with ...

The conversation might have progressed better like this (i.e., with Pat not hijacking the limelight):

Sam: I'm thinking of doing a course on mindfulness.
Pat: Oh yeah? When do you start?

The advantages of the ping-pong style (rather than the *me me me* style) for your non-native interlocutors are that they will:

- Have an opportunity to speak—and thus have some control over the conversation and also of the English vocabulary that they will use.
- Not have to concentrate on listening to you for long periods of time. Listening in another language can be very tiring.
- Participate considerably more in the conversation, and thus come away with the impression that their voice was heard and that they performed well from an English language point of view.

The result will be that the non-natives will have a positive impression of you, and this will certainly facilitate communication in the future. The *me me me* style on the other hand could lead to frustration on their part, and thus a negative picture of you.

At the other extreme, there are those non-natives who may be reluctant to speak at all. There may be two reasons for this:

1. They are worried about making mistakes (both linguistic and cultural).
2. If they are much younger than you or lower down in a company hierarchy, they may simply be showing you respect. Their education system may have taught them that they should listen rather than ask questions or contribute.

So if you find yourself talking too much, try to send the ball back into their court by asking them a question—preferably an open-ended question that cannot simply be answered with a *yes* or *no*. This will send them a clear message that you are encouraging them to talk and thus value what they have to say. Also, compliment them on their English; this will encourage them to speak up more and not be worried about making mistakes.

8.2 Are the dynamics of socializing and effective conversation the same the world over?

Think about your friends and family—do they all have the same communication style? Do they all adopt the ping-pong approach outlined in Section 8.1? Probably not. So the way we communicate is not necessarily due to where we come from.

The way we communicate, whatever our nationality or culture, may also be conditioned by:

- Our personality, for example, how curious we are about other people and how empathetic we are;
- How much we have traveled and thus been exposed to different conversation styles.

So as you do business around the world, you may find people who adopt the same conversational strategies as you or who may have a different approach. For example, you may find people who:

- Feel no obligation to introduce you to the other participants in the conversation.
- Go through a long ritual of asking you about how all the various members of your family are before they begin with any specifics about recent experiences that either of you may have had.
- Do not ask questions as a means of starting a conversation, but simply start talking about something that interests them. For such people, conversations are essentially in the form of a series of announcements, where one person says something and then another person comments or provides a new piece of information about something else.
- May view you with suspicion if you are too quick to get a conversation going. For them the idea may be that social relationships call for caution and should be given time to develop.
- Do not appreciate being bombarded with a seemingly endless series of personal questions (*so what do you do? so where do you work? so do you have any children?*).

- Tolerate long gaps in a conversation. Given our aversion to silence, this means that we may tend to fill the silences, with the result that our counterparts go away feeling that we are rather rude, even arrogant and self-centered.

The key is that you:

- Always speak clearly and slowly, constantly bearing in mind that they are doing you an enormous favor by talking to you in your language (which entails no effort for you, but may require considerable effort for them).
- Don't dominate the conversation.
- Encourage your counterparts to speak, and then show genuine interest in what they are saying.
- Don't assume that your way of conducting a conversation is necessarily the best or only way.

So far I have tried to avoid making any generalizations about specific cultures, but I can't resist the temptation of quoting from a 160-page book devoted entirely to one specific element of oral communication style in Japanese. In their wonderful book *How To Be Polite in Japanese*, Osamu and Nobuko Mizutani, make the following observations:

- When two Japanese converse, the listener frequently gives short reply words [called *aizuchi*]. They are given as a sign that the listener is listening attentively and has understood so far, and to encourage the speaker to go on. The average number of *aizuchi* per minute is around 20.
- In the English idea of conversation or dialogue, one statement is finished and then another statement follows, but in Japanese conversation, even one statement can be made up by two people.
- The Japanese regard it as good to invite the listener to give an opinion or judgment by leaving a certain point of the sentence unsaid [which the interlocutor is invited to finish].

- Expressing one's reserve by sounding hesitant is essential to being polite, perhaps even more so than using polite expressions.
- Foreign speakers of Japanese sometimes seem impolite because they tend to explain things too much. The Japanese will also give some reason, for example, for being late, but it is regarded as good to apologize first and to make the explanation as short as possible.

The Mizutanis' book highlights that we cannot take our norms of socializing for granted, and that we should try to take on board other approaches.

8.3 How careful do I need to be about using humor?

Raymond Ng, a Chinese businessman and cross cultural expert living in British Columbia, recounts an amusing anecdote, which while highlighting the Chinese concerns regarding safety hazards, draws attention to the potential pitfalls of using humor.

> One day [a realtor] showed a home to a new immigrant from Hong Kong. The house backed onto a green belt which drew the attention of the customer more than a few times. After spending a long time in the house, the customer asked if there were any coyotes in the area. The realtor replied: "You don't have to worry about coyotes. They were all eaten up by the bears." The customer disappeared in no time and the realtor never had a chance to explain it had all been meant as a harmless joke!

Interestingly, humor can vary even between the nations of the Anglosphere. A British businessman who has worked both in the Asia Pacific area and with colleagues from the United States told me:

> There are situations where the Americans don't expect humor or cynicism or even skepticism. What they expect is a very optimistic enthusiastic approach, where everybody is eagerly working together to produce some strong outcome. This is very different with the Japanese, for example, or Singaporeans and Hong Kong

groups, because they don't come at it from that point of view. Thus the experience with the Americans is more one of frustration: they don't really understand that a bit of humor might be a way of lubricating the conversation and getting the parties comfortable with each other.

American readers of this book may find it surprising that although US comedy series are loved in Britain, many British people like myself find that Americans can be quite serious and intense, and that our dry British sense of humor (often used to de-dramatize a situation) seems to be lost on them.

Humor can be a bit of a minefield. My advice would be to follow the line of your more experienced friends and colleagues—if their attempts with humor are met with a genuine smile or laughter, then you can try using some yourself. But a joke or quip that works with one nationality may not necessarily work with another. Be cautious.

8.4 How should I communicate at the restaurant?

A few fundamental rules should help you to communicate better with your foreign clients, in what for them is a rather difficult situation.

The first problem is the environment itself. Restaurants are noisy. This makes it doubly difficult for the foreigner to understand what is being said. If possible sit next to the people you need to talk to. Don't talk across the table as they simply may not be able to hear you but may not say so for fear of embarrassment.

Secondly, at the *meeting* table, your clients will know the subject under discussion and should have all the keywords at their command. At the *dining* table, conversations twist and turn at the whim of the speakers. Your clients will have little or no opportunity to control the language being used; they will be completely outside their technical area and may have very little knowledge of the terminology used in other fields such as sports, music, education, and the family.

Food is obviously a big topic at the dinner table. There are so many different foods and cooking methods that it's impossible to be familiar with them all. Help your guest by asking the waiter to bring examples of what is on the menu. Alternatively, use your phone to find an online dictionary to translate unknown words or show them photos of what the dish looks like.

Cultural elements really come into play around the dinner table too. Your guests may be unable to eat certain foods (e.g., pork or beef) or drink alcohol. You should ask them right from the beginning if they have any particular needs.

And don't take things for granted. My wife and I were once invited to dinner by an Iranian family—the father was an ex general in the Iranian army, the mother a teacher, and the son a PhD student of mine. When we sat down at the table, they asked us what we would like to drink, and in an attempt to show respect we said we would have water. They promptly ordered wine for themselves. Somewhat taken aback, we mentioned the Muslim prohibition of alcohol, to which they responded that they were all atheists.

8.5 What topics of conversation should I choose, and which should I avoid?

As in any social context, both at home and abroad, usually safe topics are food, the family, work, sightseeing, holidays, and the weather.

The secret is to let your non-native colleagues steer the conversation. This means that:

- You limit the potential of encroaching on taboo areas (politics, war, religion, racism, women's issues and sex, health, and death).
- They have the opportunity to choose a topic for which they already know the words they are going to need.
- They will naturally do more of the talking—this will make them feel good and will also take the pressure off them in trying to listen and understand your English.

When taking part in a discussion, try to focus on the areas that you have in common (whether these are personal ideas or culturally-dependent ideas) rather than the differences. If you focus on the differences this could lead to disagreement, which could have a negative impact on your future relationships.

Tushar Bansal and Veena Vishwa, two Indians who once spent many years working in Europe, have this advice about what *not* to do during a social conversation:

- Don't get too personal—do not ask much about personal relationship details of past, neither of the individual nor of his/her spouse.
- Don't ask about the problem between Hindus and Muslims (and other religious talk). If religion-based beliefs are given, they should be accepted/respected rather than counter-questioned or debated.
- Don't make a person lose face in front of a group.
- Maintain an arm's distance (don't touch the person while speaking). This is very important while speaking with the opposite sex.

Their advice works well for first dealings with practically any nationality.

8.6 What questions might I be asked? How should I deal with them?

Apart from standard questions about your nationality, your occupation, your city/town, and period of stay in their country, some nationalities might ask you about your marital status, whether you have children, your age, and your salary. Clearly, none of these types of questions are difficult to answer. However, there may be some lines of questioning that might appear to be provocative or which will raise doubts in your mind as to whether you should defend your compatriots, express a personal opinion, or simply avoid the question.

If you are American, some typical questions (or types of questions) that you might be asked by people of different nationalities are:

1. Why is there so much homelessness in America? In this day and age, how is it possible to find such wealth and poverty living side by side?

2. What battle in your opinion marked the turning point in the American war of independence?
3. Why is New York so violent?
4. Why do your newspapers contain so little international news, but so much scandal?
5. Apparently many Americans never travel abroad and can't even recognize their own country on a map of the world? Is this true?

The key factors to remember here are:

- The questioner assumes that you, being an American, must know everything about the country's history, geography, politics, and so on. I live in Italy, and when I have guests from the UK, they expect me to know the entire history of Italian art, all the names of plants and different types of bread, exactly how wine is made and all the different varieties, and a whole load of things that they would certainly not know about the UK.
- You may well have a tendency to ask similar questions to a non-native. So make sure *your* questions are based on up-to-date information and avoid questions that require some kind of specialist answer. Also, ensure that you are not encroaching on a minefield area (this requires some research before you meet your counterparts).

I asked one American whether she found it irritating when people say the United States is very insular. Her answer shows the level of frustration that many people who travel have experienced:

If you are being hosted in a country and somebody asks you one of these questions, you can't respond too truthfully because you're a guest. But at the same time, they are saying *Americans never go anywhere and* you're sitting in their front room and have a full passport with stamps from twelve different countries, and you can even read the Chinese characters on their tea set. So you want to say: well most of us who have passports have been to university and ...

Now let's look at ways of dealing with the five "difficult" questions:

1. Revert the question back: *I don't really have the answer to that question. Do you have a problem with homelessness in your country?*
2. Say you are not an expert in that field, and ask them a question on the same topic but which is easy to answer: *When did your country become independent?* Or make a related comment: *If I am not wrong, your country was once a French colony, right?*
3. Politely put the questioner right, but acknowledge that on some level they do have a point: *Actually, New York is really quite safe now. But you're right; it did use to be quite dangerous.*
4. Avoid confrontation by asking the questioner what he/she thinks is the answer to the question.
5. Make some kind of generalization or express some kind of agreement: *I think a lot of people presume that that is the case. Yes, we do have a reputation for being a bit self-focused.*

The secret is not to take questions (particularly unfair accusations) too personally. Don't feel that you are an ambassador of your country and therefore have to defend the homeland. Most people appreciate having harmony maintained, irrespective of their culture.

8.7 What are the main points that I should take away from reading this book?

In our working relations with foreign partners, the role of how we communicate in English has been severely underestimated.

The way business is conducted between companies of different nationalities is becoming more and more standard through globalization and the spread of the Internet and social media. Thus differences in culture are becoming less and less obvious and less and less decisive. But what can really differentiate you from your Anglophone competitors is recognizing your foreign counterparts' difficulties in communicating in English, and doing all in your power to render the experience as stress free as possible.

The ways to achieve this are not difficult and essentially involve following the tips outlined at the end of each chapter in this book and remembering to always put yourself in the other person's shoes. The benefit will be that your working collaborations are significantly more effective and your company will gain a competitive edge by having a reputation as promoting a highly non-native friendly communication style.

Don't assume that just because you have had what you think are effective relations with non-natives that your usual approach is necessarily the best or right one. There is always room for re-evaluation and improvement, and the strategies outlined in this book should help you to become an even better communicator.

My final suggestion would be for you to try learning another language. And when you've learned a bit of it, travel to a country where it is spoken and put it into action. In the space of less than one week you will feel the handicap of never being fully in control of the situation and the frustration, humiliation, and loss of identity that often comes with that. It is a truly humbling experience, but one that will serve you very well in the business world and the world in general.

Top Tips for Communication with Non-native English Speakers

- When dealing with other cultures, never assume that your approach is the best. Instead focus on areas that you have in common and try to move forward together rather than on separate paths.
- The key skill when socializing is to make the other person feel at ease. This sense of ease will be promoted if your interlocutor finds your English easy to understand.
- Don't let people's "unacceptable" behavior color your attitude to them. What might be unacceptable to you may be perfectly acceptable to them. And vice versa.
- Be aware that the norms of conversation vary from culture to culture: silence, not asking questions, and finishing the sentences of your interlocutor may all be acceptable (even if

it feels strange to you). Failure to recognize and respect these norms can occasionally result in unnecessary hostility.

- At the dining table, speak loudly and clearly. Explain menu items very carefully. Stick to safe topics of conversation.
- On social occasions, be aware that a non-native who is in a group of predominantly native-English speakers is likely to find the conversation difficult to follow and thus very tiring. Try to pitch your vocabulary and speed of delivery so that he/she can keep up with you.
- Try and maintain harmony in all interactions. When in doubt persevere, be patient, and above all, be respectful.
- If you adopt a friendly approach, allow a bit of time to pass, and show respect, understanding and patience, everything should fall into place. What may initially seem like an inscrutable expression on the face of your counterpart will soon soften if you take the time to get to know the person in question and show patience when listening.

Sources

Chapter 1

Eight things

(4) Education First: ef-italia.it/epi/

(6) Harvard Business Review: https://hbr.org/2012/05/global-business-speaks-english

(8) Eurostat: http://ec.europa.eu/eurostat/statistics-explained/index.php/Foreign_language_learning_statistics

1.2

Sarah Lyall. 2008. *The Anglo Files: A Field Guide to the British*. New York: W. W. Norton

Ann Marie Sabbath. 1999. *International Business Etiquette: Europe*. NJ: Career Press

Gordon Neale. 2008. *Buying a House in Italy*. Surrey (UK): Crimson Publishing

Harry King. 2006. *Spain, Your Guide to a New Life*. Oxford: How to Books

1.3 https://hbr.org/2012/05/global-business-speaks-english

Schreiber quote courtesy of Chandler Davis—personal communication. Interview with Jean-Paul Nerrière quoted in the New York Times (April 21, 2005).

1.4 Katja Kaila—personal communication

Interview with Hamish McRae conducted by Anna Southern and quoted in: Adrian Wallwork. 2002. *Business Vision*. Oxford: Oxford University Press.

1.5 Pavel Belchev—personal communication.

1.6 Courtesy of sales representative at Oxford University Press Poland.

1.10 Survey carried out by Adrian Wallwork for ION Trading, a privately held, global financial software firm.

Chapter 2

Six things:

(2) Courtesy of Mike Seymour.

(6) The Guardian: https://theguardian.com/small-business-network/
2017/jun/20/squaring-the-circle-on-jargon-why-do-we-speak-in-riddles-
at-work?CMP=Share_iOSApp_Other

2.2 Odditycentral: http://odditycentral.com/news/m-lavinashree-worlds-
youngest-computer-wiz.html

2.9 Survey carried out by Adrian Wallwork for List Group, financial software firm with head offices in Pisa, Italy.

Chapter 3

Six things

(1) Daily Mail November 18, 2011.

(2) David Bellos. 2011. *Is that a Fish in Your Ear?* London: Penguin Books.

(3) The Times April 26, 2011.

(4) Financial Times January 18, 1998.

3.2 John Donald Redmond—personal communication.

3.3 Waves produced by Tommaso Wallwork at the Nervous Horizon
studios in London.

3.4 Sue Osada—personal communication.

3.7 Staph Bakali—personal communication.

3.9 Survey conducted for List Group (see 2.9 above).

3.10 Rajiv Khan—personal communication.

3.10 The Economist:https://economist.com/blogs/johnson/2011/05/
euphemistically_speaking

Top tips

(1) Joseph O'Connor and Robin Prior. 1995. *Successful Selling with NLP.*
New York, NY: HarperCollins.

Chapter 4

Seven things

(1) Kentucky Community & Technical College System: https://
publicsearch.kctcs.edu/publication/Lists/Publications/DispForm.
aspx?ID=3484&Article=14115

(2) Ingco International: http://ingcointernational.com/the-20-most-translated-texts-in-history/

(4) Claudia Rawlins. 1973. *Business Communication*. New York, NY: HarperCollins.

(6) National Social Science Association. Kandra et al *Power Browsing: Empirical Evidence at the College Level*. http://nssa.us/tech_journal/volume_2-2/vol2-2_article4.htm

(7) Eriko Gargiulo—personal communication.

4.1 Spam email to the author.

4.3 Martin Cutts. 2009. *Oxford Guide to Plain English*. Oxford:Oxford University Press

4.4 Richard Wydick. 2005. *Plain English for Lawyers*. Carolina Academic Press.

4.8 Sample of Dzongkha kindly provided by Dr Tamang Asta Maya; information on the Bible in Italy courtesy of Professor Adriano Prosperi.

4.10 Joke provided by Richard McGowan, head of technical writing at ION Trading, explanation by James Wynne.

Tips
Oxford Dictionaries: https://en.oxforddictionaries.com/explore/how-many-words-are-there-in-the-english-language

Chapter 5

Eight things

(3) Eriko Gargiulo—personal communication.

(6) Adrian Wallwork. 1999. *Business Options*. Oxford: Oxford University Press.

(8) Tentmaker: tentmaker.org/Quotes/lawyers-per-capita.html

(9) The Guardian: theguardian.com/commentisfree/2017/sep/14/death-hope-productivity-meetingorganisations?utm_source=esp&utm_medium=Email&utm_campaign=GU+Today+main+NEW+H+-categories&utm_term=243679&subid=15225142&CMP=EMC-NEWEML6619I2

5.1 Eriko Gargiulo—personal communication.

5.2 Adrian Wallwork. 2002. *Business Vision*. Oxford: Oxford University Press.

5.3 Luciano Modica, Michelle Hopkins, and Martin Gandy—personal communications.

5.4 Responses to my question on Quora from George Fahmy and Cedric El Frangi. Sinking ship: http://i18nguy.com/adventures/whotosave. html#results

5.6 Adrian Wallwork. 1999. *Business Options*. Oxford: Oxford University Press.

5.6–5.8 Phone and face-to-face conversations with employees of ION Trading (see Section 1.10)

5.10 Christalyn Brannen. 1997. *Going to Japan on Business*. Berkeley: Stone Bridge Press.

Chapter 6

Six things

(1) BBC: bbc.com/news/technology-35038429; http://www.nbc-links. com/powerpoint.html;

(2) Richard Hall. 2007. *Brilliant Presentation*. Harlow, UK: Pearson Education.

(3) Training Mag: https://trainingmag.com/trgmag-article/2o15-training-industry-report; brain: https://forbes.com/sites/work-in-progress/2014/11/14/six-ways-to-avoid-death-by-powerpoint/3/#1b6be9ab7aa4

(4) Adrian Wallwork. 1999. *Business Options*. Oxford: Oxford University Press.

6.4 Ravindra P. Jumde and Choudhury Abul Anam Rashed—personal communications.

6.5 Don Daughter's speech appeared in: Adrian Wallwork. 1999. *Business Options*. Oxford: Oxford University Press.

Chapter 7

Seven things

(1) Alamin M Mazrui. 2016. *Cultural Politics of Translation*. NY: Routledge; Emily, A. 2005. *The Translation Zone*. NJ: Princeton University Press.

(2) Day Translations: https://daytranslations.com/mistranslations/hospital-mistranslations-the-dangers-behind-translating-intoxicado-as-intoxicated

(3) SBS News: http://sbs.com.au/news/article/2017/01/24/translators-are-struggling-interpret-donald-trump

(5) Spinoza (in Italian): http://forum.spinoza.it/viewtopic.php?f=3&t=18357&start=0

7.1 Shanshan Zhou—personal communication.

7.4 Spam email sent to the author: *Artık İngilizcesiz Olmaz*, Konuşarak Öğren, September 2017.

7.4 Banner Travel: six-degrees.com/the-high-cost-of-small-mistakes-the-most-expensive-typos-

7.6 Eileen Guo. 2012. *Afghanistan, Humor Finds Its Way in Lost Translation* published in the *New York Times*. https://atwar.blogs.nytimes.com/2012/12/04/in-afghanistan-humor-finds-its-way-in-lost-translation/of-all-time/

7.6 Some of these guidelines (from this section and the previous one) were based on an article by Sara Bird entitled *Lost Without Translation* which is available on pdf at: yooyahcloud.com/SARHN/tyeaO/AFP_Lost_without_translation.pdf and which lists several 'risk management strategies'

Chapter 8

Seven things

(1) Christopher Hill. 1987. *The English. A Social History 1066–1945*. UK: Grafton Books.

(7) Private Eye: https://theguardian.com/media/2017/nov/05/inside-world-private-eye-cartoonists-brutal-competition-jokes?CMP=Share_iOSApp_Other

8.1 Charles Derber. 2000. *The Pursuit of Attention*. Oxford: Oxford University Press.

8.2 Osamu Mizutani and Nobuko Mizutani. 1989. *Japan: How to be Polite in Japanese*. Tokyo: The Japan Times.

8.2 Asia Pacific information: Tom Southern—personal communication.

8.3 Raymond Ng. 1996. *Customers from Afar*. Vancouver: A Success Publication.

Index

www.ingramcontent.com/pod-product-compliance
Lightning Source LLC
Chambersburg PA
CBHW050113210326
41519CB00015BA/3941